LETTERS FROM THE WEST

LETTERS FROM THE WEST;

CONTAINING

SKETCHES OF SCENERY, MANNERS, AND CUSTOMS;

AND ANECDOTES CONNECTED WITH THE

FIRST SETTLEMENTS OF THE WESTERN SECTIONS OF THE UNITED STATES
(1828)

BY

JAMES HALL

A FACSIMILE REPRODUCTION

WITH AN INTRODUCTION

BY

JOHN T. FLANAGAN

GAINESVILLE, FLORIDA
SCHOLARS' FACSIMILES & REPRINTS
1967

SCHOLARS' FACSIMILES & REPRINTS
1605 N.W. 14TH AVENUE
GAINESVILLE, FLORIDA, 32601 U.S.A.
HARRY R. WARFEL, GENERAL EDITOR

L.C. CATALOG CARD NUMBER: 67-10123

MANUFACTURED IN THE U.S.A.

INTRODUCTION

The Ohio River lured many travellers westward in the early 1800's. Not to mention the boatload of knowledge which disembarked at Robert Owen's New Harmony colony in 1825, the great fluvial road to the Mississippi beckoned to the missionary Timothy Flint, the ornithologist Audubon, the Swedenborgian horticulturist Johnny Appleseed, the naturalist Rafinesque, and a little later to visiting Britons like Charles Dickens and Sir Charles Lyell. On the southern side of the Ohio River, Kentucky had become a state as early as 1792; on the northern side Ohio joined the Federal Union in 1803 and Indiana in 1816 and Illinois in 1818. But back of the river much of the territory remained wild and primitive with sporadic settlements on the tributary streams and muddy traces linking the hamlets and villages hewn out of the forest. It is true that by the end of the first quarter of the century most of the Indians had dis-

v

appeared. But wild beasts remained, road agents and river pirates were not unknown, and Mike Fink was still king of the keelboatmen. To a man in quest of adventure, eager to ride the wilderness trails, exhume Indian mounds, share the rough life of the taverns and groggeries, the Ohio Valley was excitingly attractive. Towns were growing rapidly and it was easy to initiate professional careers. The transmontane West was the symbol of opportunity.

I

In 1820 James Hall was twenty-six, a veteran of the War of 1812, a professional ordnance officer who had resigned from the service to study law at Pittsburgh, a member of a prominent Philadelphia family long active in legal and journalistic circles. His mother Sarah Ewing Hall wrote prose and verse; his brother John Elihu Hall succeeded Joseph Dennie as the editor of the *Port Folio*, a Philadelphia literary magazine which attained both distinction and unusual longevity in early federal America. James Hall himself wrote verse at an early age and penned several sketches of military life deriving from his experiences in the Niagara Campaign. By the time he resolved to voyage down the Ohio River on a keelboat, he had sampled several professions and was well prepared to cope with the challenges and opportunities of the western

country. The struggling river settlement of Shawneetown was for him the port of entry to a new society.

Hall remained in the Ohio Valley for the rest
of his life, but after some twelve years in Illinois
he backtracked to Cincinnati, where he arrived
early in 1833. In Illinois he resided in Shawneetown and Vandalia; he practiced law, served as
prosecuting attorney and district judge, edited the
Illinois Gazette, the second newspaper to be established in the state, compiled the *Western Souvenir,*
the first western literary annual, edited and published the *Illinois Monthly Magazine,* and served as
state treasurer for four years (1827-1831). In Cincinnati he continued his career as editor and writer
but combined with these activities an interest in
banking and was for many years the cashier of
the Commercial Bank. He died at his country
home in the outskirts of the city in 1868.

Despite his extraordinary versatility Hall was
primarily a literary man, a literary pioneer of the
Ohio Valley and a spokesman for the region which
he had adopted as his home. For some thirty years
he produced editorials, stories, verse, and fiction.
He is the author of a book of travels, of one novel,
of several collections of short tales, of various
statistical compilations of financial and economic
data, of the text of a sumptuous pictorial gallery of

the American Indian, and of *The Romance of Western History* (1857), an interpretation of the settlement of the Ohio Valley.

II

Letters from the West was published as a book
by the London firm of Henry Colburn in 1828. Up
to the present time it has never had an American
edition. Indeed the appearance of these letters in
book form at all was somewhat fortuitous. Some of
them are actually twice-told tales.

Several of the letters appeared originally in
the *Illinois Gazette* in the fall of 1820. Some were
printed in the *Port Folio* between December, 1821,
and March, 1825. According to an editorial note in
the twelfth volume of the *Port Folio*, September,
1821, "The preceding letters from the pen of one
of our former correspondents, were originally intended for a Western Newspaper in which a few of
them appeared, but the writer having enlarged his
design, determined, at our request, to publish the
series in the Port Folio. He has desired us to state
that they are written under the pressure of ill health
and much business: he therefore claims a candid
judgment." Then, as Hall himself stated somewhat
embarrassedly in a manuscript autobiographical
sketch, he gave the materials to a friend bound for
England in the hope that eventually they would

reach a London publisher. Hall himself lost track
of the manuscript for some time, had no opportunity to revise or read proof, and to his consterna-
tion found the volume which he had written as a
light-hearted account of a western journey suddenly
appearing in the guise of a learned treatise on the
new world written by a western jurist. The title
page actually carried the author's name as "the
Hon. Judge Hall."

The twenty-two letters which made up the
1828 English edition may be divided into two parts.
On May 6, 1820, Hall reached his destination,
Shawneetown, Illinois, and left his keelboat. The
first twelve letters, except for the digression in Letter Eight where Hall gives the biography of Gen.
Presby Neville, concern primarily his personal ex
periences on the river, the scenery along the Ohio,
the various kinds of boats encountered, characteri-
zations of both immigrants and boatmen, conditions of travel, descriptions of human and animal
life ashore, anecdotes and fragments of balladry
heard en route. Once on land at Shawneetown, Hall
pictures his new residence in some detail and attempts to discount some of the vilification of the climate and the annual freshets. But most of the rest
of the book consists of rather lengthy and often
diffuse essays on whatever Hall found of interest in
the western country, its history, its legendry, its

topography, the character of its people. Here are
inserted the accounts of Daniel Boone, Hugh Glass,
and the nefarious Harpes. Here too Hall general-
ized on popular superstitions, place names, and the
motives and goals of emigration.

He who knows the Ohio River today will of
course miss some of the things familiar to Hall a
hundred and forty-five years ago. The barge has
replaced the keelboat or flatboat, and the starling
has no doubt supplanted the bright green parra-
keets which today are virtually extinct. A century
of industrialism has contaminated the water, so
that La belle Rivière of the French boatmen is unfortunately no longer so clean and so fresh as they
had found it. The rapidity of fluvial traffic does not
permit a man to wander ashore with a shotgun in
pursuit of squirrels while his slowly drifting keel-
boat rounds a sandy point. Nor do snatches of old
ballads linger in the air as tugs and scows lumber
past. But civilization has not changed the head-
lands, diminished the bluffs, or even dulled the
foliage: gum and dogwood and redbud still dash
the spring with color. And some of the place names
that fascinated Hall by their singularity or historical appropriateness still remain on the map.

Although the order of treatment is casual
and many subjects are linked by association rather

than by strict logic, the tone of the book is remarkably consistent. Indeed *Letters from the West*
possesses a charm, an insouciance, almost at times
a flippancy that is rare in early western travel
narratives. Although imperfectly educated, Hall
was a literate man who bore his reading lightly.
His allusions to Shakespeare, Sterne, and Walter
Scott are natural and sincere. He refers to Shylock,
Roderick Dhu, FitzJames, and Dr. Pangloss because these characters are part of his literary heri-
tage, not dragged in for literary effect. He quotes
from Tom Moore and Goldsmith as easily as he
does from the Bible.

Hall's style, moreover, reveals pleasant vari-
ations. He can utilize puns and quibbles. He can
employ rhetoric self-consciously, as when he writes
that "the gall of political enmity has been infused
into the cup of social intercourse," or describes
the spring in terms of the forest "rapidly discarding
the dark and dusky habiliments of winter" and
"assuming its vernal robes." He can protest mildly
against indictments of his new home: "Shawnee
Town is never overflowed by ordinary floods." And
he can also admit that the fall mosquitoes are dissipated insects, "frolicking all night, and sleeping
all day." Moreover, they are "muscular and
sprightly, with a good appetite and sharp teeth."

Certainly Hall's descriptions of landscapes and people have both point and precision.

On the other hand, *Letters from the West* is not unmarked by seriousness. Experience had brought Hall knowledge of the western people; he valued their friendliness, their self-reliance, their hospitality, their candor. At times he was exaggeratedly patriotic, even chauvinistic. He resented English aspersions on the American scene, and he repudiated some of Mrs. Trollope's diatribes about the coarseness of western manners even before she printed them in *Domestic Manners of the Americans*, 1832. Of English and Scotch-Irish stock himself, Hall had the westerner's resentment of the patronizing tone of British visitors to the United States. On the very last page of his book he pointed out that if English travellers objected to American taverns, it was often because the taverns were actually kept by slovenly, dissolute immigrants from the British Isles. Sensitive to criticism from foreigners, Hall felt that there was no need for the pot to call the kettle black.

III

As an obscure young author James Hall probably did not expect widespread attention to his first important book. In actual fact the reviews were sparse and in one case hostile. The *New Monthly Magazine* for December, 1828, described *Letters from the West* as elegant and even amusing but voiced objections to Hall's rather florid style. Calling attention to the author's nationality and pointing out that the descriptions of western life often revealed a kind of semi-barbarous existence, the magazine derided the story of Daniel Boone as being lacking in romance, felt that the inclusion of the account of the Harpes displayed bad taste, and of course objected to the denigration of the English. The reviewer might have been even more tart save for the fact that the *New Monthly Magazine* was the property of Henry Colburn, the publisher of Hall's book. On the other hand, the *London Quarterly Review* for April, 1829, minced no words. John Barrow, the critic, asserted that Hall lied about the merits of the western climate, denied him any virtues whatever as an observer either of scene or inhabitants, and hotly resented the author's Anglophobia. Barrow summarized his censure by calling the volume a silly book and by terming its creator a judicial blockhead.

No substantial American magazine reviewed *Letters from the West*. The *North American Review* for July, 1829, listed the volume under its "Miscellaneous New Books": "*Letters from the West;*

containing Sketches of Scenery, Manners, and Customs. By the Hon. Judge Hall, Jr." But the magazine gave neither place nor date of publication and otherwise ignored it. On the other hand, the *Museum of Foreign Literature and Science*, published by the Littell firm in Philadelphia, announced the book, giving the complete title, in its issue of January, 1829. The initial pages of the April, 1829 number (Volume XIV, pp. 289-294) were given over to a reprinting of most of the *Monthly Review* notice, including the extensive quotations. Timothy Flint, Hall's rival editor in Cincinnati, alluded to Hall in his survey of western writers in the *Western Monthly Review* for June, 1828, and later reviewed other Hall books in the *Knickerbocker*, which he edited briefly in 1833, and in the *London Athenaeum*, but overlooked *Letters from the West*. Except for incidental newspaper references, the book seems to have escaped notice by the American periodical press.

When Evert and George Duyckinck compiled their *Cyclopaedia of American Literature* in 1855, they devoted over five pages to a sketch of Hall with ample quotations from his works. *Letters from the West* was described as a work "written in the character of a youth travelling for amusement, giving the rein to a lively fancy, and indulging a vein of levity and rather extravagant fun." The

Duyckinks were quite aware of the misconceptions held by the English reviewers and rightly attributed Hall's failure to allow another edition to appear to the strictures of the British press.

Much later, in 1925, Ralph Leslie Rusk in his study of the literature of the middlewestern frontier singled out Hall as the most important and most influential of the early writers of the region and frequently quoted Hall's remarks on the manners, customs, and language of the Ohio Valley as valid and perceptive observation. Social historians of the twentieth century have reached a similar conclusion about the significance of Hall as a contemporary observer.

Today's reader of *Letters from the West,* however, need have no such serious intent. As a variegated travelogue, as a series of casual sketches of a young adventurer exposed to a strange new world, as the revelation of a buoyant personality, the book can stand on its own feet. Hall was certainly no Charles Doughty, no John Ledyard, no Sir Richard Burton. But he made the Ohio Valley of the 1820's come alive. An American edition of *Letters from the West* seems amply justified.

JOHN T. FLANAGAN

University of Illinois
March 8, 1966

LETTERS FROM THE WEST;

CONTAINING

SKETCHES

OF

SCENERY, MANNERS, AND CUSTOMS;

AND ANECDOTES CONNECTED WITH THE

FIRST SETTLEMENTS OF THE WESTERN SECTIONS

OF THE

UNITED STATES.

BY THE HON. JUDGE HALL.

LONDON:

HENRY COLBURN, NEW BURLINGTON STREET.

1828.

LONDON:

SHACKELL AND BAYLIS, JOHNSON'S-COURT, FLEET-STREET.

PREFACE.

THE following Letters were commenced in the year 1820, and were intended for the pages of a periodical work,* in which some of them have been published. A residence of several years in the country which he attempts to describe, has enabled the author to enlarge his original plan, and to offer the result of his observations in the more formidable shape of a volume— formidable to the public, who are already sur- feited with books, and to the author, who in this dress, may incur the test of criticism, which he might have escaped under the humbler garb of a periodical writer.

---

* THE PORTFOLIO, a monthly magazine, which has been published at Philadelphia since the year 1801—a degree of lon- gevity altogether unequalled in the United States. It is con- ducted by John E. Hall, Esq., who is likewise the editor of an " American Law Journal," and other works on Jurisprudence.

It will be seen that neither a history nor a book of travels is attempted, but a mere collection of sketches, with but little choice of subjects, and still less attention to the order in which they are arranged. If his work should afford amusement, the author will be satisfied ; if it should develope any new fact, honourable to his country, or useful to its citizens, his highest aim will be achieved ; and, in any event, he will submit cheerfully to the verdict of public opinion, convinced that his book, if too dull to deserve approbation, is too brief to merit censure.

CONTENTS.

LETTERS FROM THE WEST.

LETTER I.

INTRODUCTORY.

CAN you tell me, my dear N——e, why I left you in sadness, though I would fain have chased away the cloud that hung upon my brow? If you can, you will explain a feeling which I have often experienced, but never could exactly define. I have seldom left a spot, at which I had sojourned long enough to form acquaintances, without a heavy heart; and yet there is something in that same heart which makes me delight to be ever roving from scene to scene. The prospect of a journey fills my

B

mind with delightful anticipations, and there is no labour which I undertake with so much alacrity as that which is preparatory to a change of place. The horse is my favourite among quadrupeds, and I find no music so inspiriting as the cracking of a coachman's whip; even the creaking of cordage, and the howling of the ocean blast, though they intimate danger, have often charmed me into forgetfulness, by harmonizing with my locomotive propensities. And yet there is a sadness in the word "farewell"—a melancholy in the glance which the traveller throws back at the receding landscape, but little in accordance with the bright visions which illumine his onward path. What is it that chains the heart to a narrow spot, when the wide world is blooming around? Can it be *fondness* for the scene which has already been enjoyed to satiety, where every thing has become monotonous, and the palled senses must feed upon the food they have grown tired of? Can it be *regret*, when pleasure allures in the perspective, and when any dear object which is left behind will be regained, and glow with new charms after a temporary absence? These are questions which you may answer if you please, for I assure you I shall not take the trouble to investigate them; it is enough for me to leave my friends with heaviness, and to return to them with delight, without intruding on philosophic ground to analyze the light and shade of those conflicting emotions, of which the experience is sufficiently pleasurable.

Now, while you are answering my questions, I will reply to yours. You ask me, in the very spirit of Goldsmith's Hermit, what allures me to " tempt the dangerous gloom," and to risk my neck, aye, and my complexion too, among the tangled forests and sun-burnt prairies of the West? I might reply, in my usual style, by a quotation from a favourite author :

" We may roam through this world like a child at a feast,
Who but sips of a sweet, and then flies to the rest ;
And when pleasure begins to grow dull in the *east*,
We may order our wings and be off to the *west* ;"—

or I might briefly say, with the churlish Shylock, " It is my humour." But as I would have you to know, that I am not so much of a knight-errant as to seek for giants for the mere pleasure of overcoming them, nor so sentimental as to hie me to purling streams and spreading shades, to cool my blood and warm my fancy, I will discuss my reasons in sober prose.

My desire of exploring the western country has not been altogether the effect of that wandering disposition to which my friends have been good enough to attribute it. It is true, too true, perhaps, that a roving fancy, indulged and confirmed into habit by the unsettled manner of my early life, may have had much weight in forming my determination; but it is equally true, that this is a national trait, entailed in common upon most of my countrymen, few of whom regard time or space, when profit or amusement allures to distant regions. But I found my strongest inducement in the deep interest we all feel in those young states which have sprung up in the wilderness, and which, expanding with unexampled rapidity, are fast becoming the rivals of their elder sisters in the east.

It might be questioned whether I have reached the years of discretion; and yet, young as I am, I can remember the time when Pitts-

burgh was considered as one of the outposts
of civilized America; and I shall never forget
the intense interest which I felt, while a boy, in
gazing at the brawny limbs and sun-burnt
features of a Kentuckian, as he passed through
the streets of Philadelphia. The rough, hardy
air of the stranger, the jaded paces of his
nag, the blanket, bear-skin, and saddle-bags—
nay, the very oil-cloth on his hat, and the dirk
that peeped from among his vestments, are still
in my eye; they bespoke him to be of distant
regions, to have been reared among dangers,
and to be familiar with fatigues. He strode
among us with the step of an Achilles, glancing
with a good-natured superciliousness at the
fragile butterflies of fashion that glittered in
the sun-beams around him. I thought I could
see in that man, one of the progenitors of an
unconquerable race; his face presented the
traces of a spirit quick to resent—he had the
will to dare, and the power to execute; there
was a something in his look which bespoke a
disdain of controul, and an absence of con-
straint in all his movements, indicating an
habitual independence of thought and action.

Such was the stock from which a new people were to spring; but the oak has blossomed and borne fruit. Science and refinement, engrafted upon the rude stem, have flourished, and have mingled their verdure and their sweets among its hardy branches. That " lone, wayfaring man," is not now the only representative of his country; the West has already sent us the statesman, upon whose accents listening thousands have hung enraptured—the gentleman, whose politeness pleases—and the maiden, whose loveliness delights us.

At the period to which I have alluded, a journey from Philadelphia to Pittsburgh was a most serious affair; and he who would adventure further, took with him arms, and guides, and provisions, and "all appliances and means to boot," necessary for subsistence and defence. What was then the goal, is now the starting place; Pittsburgh is the threshold by which we pass into the great States of the West; and Kentucky, but lately a *western* frontier, is now one of the *eastern* boundaries of the western country.

The shores of the Mississippi, and its tribu-

tary streams, present to the world a singular
and most enchanting picture—one which future
ages will contemplate with wonder and delight.
The celerity with which the soil has been
peopled, and the harmony which has prevailed
in the erection of their governments, have no
parallel in history, and seem to be the effect of
magic, rather than of human agency. Europe
was at one time overrun by numerous hordes,
who, rushing like a torrent from the North, in
search of a more genial climate, captured or
expelled the effeminate inhabitants of the South,
and planted colonies in its richest provinces;
but these were savages, who conquered with the
sword, and ruled with the rod of iron. The
"arm of flesh" was visible in all their operations. Their colonies, like ours, were formed by
emigration ; the soil was peopled with an exotic
population; but here the parallel ends. The
country, gained by violence, was held by force ;
the blood-stained soil produced nothing but
"man and steel, the soldier and his sword."

What a contrast does our happy country
present to scenes like these ! It remained for us
to exhibit to the world the novel spectacle of

a people, coming from various nations, and
differing in language, politics, and religion,
sitting down quietly together, erecting states,
forming constitutions, and enacting laws,
without bloodshed or dissension. Our curiosity
is excited to know what powerful attraction has
drawn these multitudes from their native plains,
and why, like bees, they swarm as it were to the
same bough. Nor is it less interesting to inquire
by what process such heterogeneous particles
have become united, and to observe the effect
of so extraordinary a combination. Is it not
singular to behold the Englishman and the
Frenchman rushing to the same goal; the laborious, economical New Englander treading the
same path with the high-minded, luxurious
native of the South; and the cautious Hollander,
with an enterprise foreign to his nature, rearing
his vine and his fig-tree at a spot whence the
footsteps of the savage aborigines are scarcely
yet effaced? Is it not more strange that such
men can live in fellowship, act in unison, make
laws in peace, and " do all things which are
requisite and necessary, as well for the body as
the soul," in harmonious concert? These are

healthful symptoms, indicating moral beauty and political soundness. With such practical effects of liberty before us, we may smile at the sneers of those, who know freedom only in theory, and, hugging their own base chains, affect to scorn that blessing which they have not the manliness to attain, or the virtue to preserve.

But there are other considerations, besides those of a political nature, which render this country peculiarly interesting. It is the refuge of thousands, who have fled from poverty, from tyranny, and from fanaticism. The tumults of Europe have driven hither crowds of unhappy beings, whose homes have been rendered odious or unsafe by the mad ambition of a few aspiring sovereigns. Here is no Holy Alliance, trafficking in human blood ; no sceptre to be obeyed, no mitre to be worshipped. Here they find not merely a shelter from the rude storm that pelts them, but they become proprietors of the soil, and citizens in the state. Here they learn the practical value of that liberty, which they only knew before in theory. They learn here, that although the Englishman may be *born a freeman*, the American only is *bred a freeman ;* the latter has this blessing in possession, while the former cherishes a vague tradition of its achievement, which is contradicted by the records of his country, and the practice of his rulers. You are not to suppose, however, that this is a land of radicals and paupers. Far from it : though many emigrate from necessity, a larger number do so from inclination. Among the emigrants are gentlemen of wealth and education, whose object is to build up estates for their children, in a country which offers such facilities for the accumulation of property, and presents so fair a promise to posterity. By far the greatest class are neither wealthy nor poor; these are respectable farmers and mechanics, who, in the present unpropitious times, find it to their interest to seek out a residence, where their labours will yield more profit than at home.

There are also a variety of historical and literary facts, connected with this country, which serve to give it interest in the eyes of an American. Braddock was defeated, and Washington immortalized, on the romantic

shores of Monongahela; and the vicinity of
Pittsburgh, already famous for the loveliness of
its mountain scenery, and the magnitude of its
mineral treasures, has been the scene of martial
achievement, which may one day wake the
lyre of the Pennsylvania bard to strains as
national and as sweet as those of Scott.   In
the western forests did Wayne gather a wreath
of imperishable laurel; and St. Clair—I blush
to name him, injured man!—a crown of thorns.
On the borders of the Ohio, Butler fell, in the
prime of his life, and the vigour of his ambition,
leaving a name which his countrymen have
delighted to embalm.   Can we trace with
indifference the path of Burr, the smoothest of
seducers, but himself seduced by the wildest of
all visionary schemes? or pass, without a tear of
sympathy, the spot, where the philosophic
Blannerhasset, surrounded in his loved seclusion
with rural and literary enjoyments, tasted of
" that peace, which the world cannot give"—
tasted, alas! for but a moment, and dashed
away?   Will it not be delightful to stray along
those shores where Wilson strayed—to view
the scenes which charmed his poetic fancy—

to mark the plumage, and listen to the " wood-
notes wild" which allured him through many a
weary mile? Surely this is classic ground,
which has been trodden by the erudite and the
brave, whose graves have been battle fields,
and in whose soil the patriot soldier reposes
from his labours!

Who has not heard of the *Antiquities of the
West?* Who that has heard, has not listened
with admiration or incredulity? Of all that
has been written on this most interesting subject, how little has appeared to satisfy a reasonable mind. The time was, when the tales
of western travellers were received as fanciful
productions, written to amuse the idle, or to
beguile the unwary emigrant into the fangs of
speculating avarice. When we were told of the
Great Valley, whose noble rivers, stretching in
every direction from the distant mountains,
poured their waters into the bosom of the
Father of Streams; and of the rich bottoms,
extensive prairies, and gigantic forests of the
West, we could smile at what we believed to
be simple exaggeration. But when we heard
of caverns, extending horizontally for miles, and

exhibiting traces of former inhabitants, of immense mausoleums filled with human bones, some of them of a dwarfish size, indicating the former existence of a pigmy race—of the skeletons of gigantic brutes—of metallic ornaments, warlike implements, and earthen utensils found buried in the soil—of the vestiges of temples and fortifications—in short, of the many remains of a civilized population, we were inclined to consider them as gross impostures. Yet these curiosities actually exist, as well as others of equal interest ; and while we can no longer withhold our credence, we cannot help exclaiming,

> "——Can such things be,
> And overcome us like a summer cloud,
> Without our special wonder!"

Are you answered now? Is not here sufficient food for speculation? Will it not be gratifying to mingle with the mighty flood which is sweeping onward to the West—to see it prostrating the forest, and depositing the seeds of art and refinement? The spots which I shall visit have not been consecrated by the

classic pen ; a Homer has not sung their
heroes, nor an Ovid peopled their shades with
divinities.   But shall I not stroll among the
ruins of ancient cities, and recline upon the
tombs of departed heroes ?   You may not admire my taste ; but, believe me, I should tread
with as much reverence over the mausoleum
of a Shawanee chief, as among the catacombs
of Egypt ; and would speculate with as much
delight on the site of an Indian village, as in
the gardens of Tivoli or the ruins of Herculaneum.

But, to add another and a last inducement,
there has been a material variance in the evidence given of this country, by the travellers
and writers who have undertaken to describe
it.   Some laud it as a paradise, others denounce
it as a hell.   Some have given it health, fertility, and commercial advantages ; others have
filled it with swamps, agues, tomahawks, and
musquitoes.   One writer tells us, that "a dirk
is the inseparable companion of every gentleman in Illinois ;" while another facetiously
hints that the *ladies* of Kentucky conceal the
same weapon among the folds of their graceful

vestments.   This latter insinuation, however,
I take to be a metaphorical compliment to the
lovely daughters of Kentucky, believing, as I
do, that the gentleman, alluding to the well-
known words of Romeo, intended to say,
" There is more peril in those eyes, than twenty
of their dirks."   I could refer you to a thousand other vile discrepancies, but I have not
room.

" I will see into it," said Mr. Shandy, when
he went to France, to learn whether they
" ordered things better" there than at home—
" I will see into it," said I, when I found how
doctors disagreed about a section of my native
country ; and it is in conformance with this
determination that I am now fairly embarked,
and gliding merrily down the Ohio.

LETTER II.

PITTSBURGH, AND ITS VICINITY.

As I commenced my tour at Pittsburgh, it may not be improper to begin my observations with a description of this thriving town. To you, to whom these details will be familiar, this may seem a superfluous task ; but as it is not a novel thing for travellers to write what is already known to their readers, I shall, at least, be able to plead numerous precedents in excuse for troubling you with a twice-told tale. The vanity of every writer—and authors are not apt to be deficient in this quality—whispers him that he can detail what he sees more agreeably than his predecessors ; while indolence, pointing out the intricate mazes that lie before him, allures the tourist, in the outset of his journey, to linger in beaten paths. You are welcome, therefore, to attribute my plagiarisms to either of these causes, remembering always, that when I promised, like Dogberry, to " bestow all my tediousness upon you," I reserved to myself the privilege of choosing the subjects of discussion.

The situation of Pittsburgh, at the head of the Ohio, and at the confluence of the Monongahela and Allegheny rivers, was probably first noticed for its military, rather than its commercial advantages. The early French and English settlers of this hemisphere of ours, were engaged in continual wars with each other, and with the natives; in the course of which, the former determined to establish a chain of posts from Canada to Louisiana. One of the most important of these was *Fort Du Quesne*, situated at this point. It did not escape the military eye of Washington, when he visited this country several years before the revolution, on a mission from the government of Virginia; and, in his despatches, he spoke of its importance with a prophetic spirit. During the struggle, which is commonly called " Braddock's war," Fort Du Quesne changed masters, and the English,

c

abandoning the original work, which was probably a mere stockade, built a more regular
fortification on a site immediately adjoining,
which they named *Fort Pitt*. This post, erected
on a low point of land, and commanded by hills
on every side, would appear to a soldier of the
present day to have been untenable, and consequently useless; nor can the reasons of its
original establishment, and subsequent importance, be ascertained, without recurring to the
history of those times. As a place of deposit
for military stores it possessed singular advantages, in the facilities which it afforded for their
transportation, as there is no other spot from
which they could have been distributed with
equal celerity, or over so large an extent of
country. Nor was its situation with regard
to defence so desperate as we might at first
imagine. It is to be recollected, that in those
days there was little or no artillery west of the
mountains; and that it was considered as almost
impossible to pass the Allegheny ridge with a
carriage of any description. There was little
reason to apprehend that any ordnance would
be brought to assail the ramparts of that insu-

lated fortress, which seemed destined to assert
the sway of Britain over a boundless wilderness. But, notwithstanding this imaginary security, the works, of which there are extensive
ruins still visible, seem to have been built after
the usual fashion of that period, and to have
had the strength, as well as the form, of a regular fortification. A bomb-proof magazine is
still extant, in good preservation. This fort is
said to have been built by Lord Stanwin, and
to have cost the British government *sixty
thousand pounds sterling.* As it would seem, by
placing it at this exposed spot, that an attack
by artillery was not apprehended, and as, if such
an attack had been made, resistance would have
been in vain, it is difficult to conceive what
could have been the motives of the builders in
giving it such strength and regularity. We
must either suppose that their military habits
prevailed over the better dictates of prudence,
or that they intended to impress their Indian
neighbours with an exalted opinion of their
security and power. It is said, that shortly
after the English took possession, the Indian
traders built a row of fine brick houses, on the

margin of the Allegheny, but that their founda-
tions were sapped by the encroachments of the
river : no vestige of them remains. About the
year 1760, a small town was built near Fort
Pitt, which contained nearly two hundred
souls ; but on the breaking out of the Indian
war in 1763, the inhabitants retired into the
fort, and their dwellings were suffered to fall
into decay. The British officers had some fine
gardens here, called the " King's," and " Artillery gardens," and large orchards of choice
fruit : the old inhabitants of the present town
recollect them ; but there are now no remains
of these early attempts at luxury and comfort.

After Fort Pitt came into the possession of
the Americans, it was occupied but for a short
time, when the garrison was removed to a spot
about a mile further up, on the Allegheny river,
where a picket work and block-houses were
erected, and called *Fort Fayette*. This post
was occupied by the United States' troops until
the erection, within a few years past, of the
arsenal, two miles further up. The location of
the arsenal as a military post is injudicious ; and
so little skill was exerted in its erection, as to

render it not susceptible of defence; but in other respects it is a convenient and valuable establishment, well calculated for the manufacture and deposit of ordnance, small arms, and other munitions of war.

Pittsburgh was first laid out in the year 1765; it was afterwards laid out, surveyed, and completed on its present plan, in 1784, by Colonel George Woods, by order of Tench Francis, Esq., attorney for John Penn, and John Penn, junior. The increase of the town was not rapid until the year 1793, in consequence of the inroads of the savage tribes, which impeded the growth of the neighbouring settlements. The western insurrection, more generally known as the "Whisky War," once more made this the scene of commotion, and is said to have given Pittsburgh a new and reviving impulse, by throwing a considerable sum of money into circulation. Since that time it has increased rapidly, and a few years ago was erected into a city.

Pittsburgh and its vicinity may proudly challenge comparison in beauty of scenery and healthfulness of situation. Surrounded by hills

and vallies which, in the seasons of verdure, are
clothed in the richest vegetation, commanding
points may be found in every direction, from
which the eye is delighted with the most
romantic scenes. Three noble streams contribute to diversify the prospect, embellishing and
enlivening an endless variety of Nature's
loveliest pictures.

Grant's-hill, an abrupt eminence which projects into the rear of the city, affords one of the
most delightful prospects with which I am acquainted ; presenting a singular combination of
the bustle of the town, with the solitude and
sweetness of the country. How many hours
have I spent here, in the enjoyment of those
exquisite sensations which are awakened by
pleasing associations and picturesque scenes!
The city lay beneath me, enveloped in smoke—
the clang of hammers resounded from its numerous manufactories—the rattling of carriages
and the hum of men were heard from its streets
—churches, courts, hotels, and markets, and all
the " pomp and circumstance" of busy life,
were presented in one panoramic view. Behind
me were all the silent soft attractions of rural

sweetness—the ground rising gradually for a considerable distance, and exhibiting country seats, surrounded with cultivated fields, gardens, and orchards. On either hand were the rivers, one dashing over beds of rock, the other sluggishly meandering among the hills;—while the lofty eminences beyond them, covered with timber, displayed a rich foliage, decked and shadowed with every tint of the rainbow. Below the town, the Ohio is seen, receiving her tributary streams, and bearing off to the west, burthened with rich freights. The towns of Allegheny on the right hand, and Birmingham on the left—the noble bridges that lead to the city in opposite directions—the arsenal, and the little village of Laurenceville, in the rear, added variety to the scene. What a spot for a poet! But little more than half a century ago, how lonely and insulated were these solitudes! How solitary was that fortress, whose flag, like an exotic flower, displayed its gaudy colours in an uncongenial clime, and whose morning gun awakened the echoes which had slept for unnumbered years! The sentry walked " his lonely round" upon those battlements which are now

in ruins—the officer strayed pensively along the
margin of the river, and as he gazed upon the
surrounding beauties, which now began to pall
upon the senses, he thought, as the poet has
since sung :

> " Society, friendship, and love,
> Divinely bestow'd upon man—
> Oh, had I the wings of a dove,
> How soon would I taste you again !"

The deer then tenanted the forest, and the
Indian with his light canoe sported on the
wave. Behold now the contrast ! But enough
of this. This eminence received its name from
Colonel Grant, a Scottish officer, who fell a
sacrifice here to his imprudent courage in the
war which ended in 1763. He had been detached with a body of eight hundred highlanders, to surprise the French garrison of Fort
Du Quesne ; and arriving at these heights in the
evening, he delayed the final blow until the
succeeding morning. The morning found him
ready for action and confident of success ; but,
elated by the impunity which had so far attended his enterprise, or despising the inactive
foe, who seemed already within his grasp,—in a

fatal moment of incaution, he ordered his musicians to sound the *réveillé*. As the martial sounds stole along the hills, calling forth the echoes from an hundred caverns, the gallant Scots might have fancied themselves in that *far awa'* land which a Scotsman never forgets ; but alas ! those bugle blasts which aroused their hearts to enthusiasm, were the last they were destined to hear ! The French and Indians, thus apprised by their enemy of his approach, sallied privately from the fort, possessed themselves of the hills in the rear of Grant, and of the surrounding coverts, and, rushing in upon the devoted party, hewed them in pieces !

Castlemain's-hill, one of the highest points in this vicinity, affords a rich and extensive prospect, embracing a view of this lovely country for many miles round. The Monongahela is seen winding its serpentine course far beneath the spectator's feet, and the city, dwindled to an atom, appears in distant perspective. Persons of taste resort to this spot, and a stranger would hardly be pardonable who should omit to pay it a visit.

Twelve miles from Pittsburgh, on the banks

of the Monongahela, is " Braddock's Field," a
scene of signal disaster to the British arms.
The name of Braddock has not been cherished
by his countrymen, and no attempt has been
made to rescue his fame from obloquy ; perhaps, because no plausible ground of vindica-
tion exists ; but every feeling mind must deplore
the premature fall of a brave, though obstinate
leader, and the sacrifice of a gallant army.
There is nothing more arbitrary than the meed
of applause or opprobrium, bestowed upon the
soldier's toils ; success being, too generally, the
test of merit. I am therefore disposed to judge
charitably of military miscarriages, and to vene-
rate the fallen brave, although they may have
fallen unwisely. He who gives his life to his
country, gives his all, and having thus proved
the sincerity of his patriotism, leaves his name
to posterity, with a sacred and imposing claim
upon their candour. In the tempest of that
day, which consigned Braddock to an un-
honoured grave, the genius of Washington
dawned, with a lustre which gave promise of its
future greatness ; and the American reveres
the spot which has been hallowed by the illus-

trious presence and gallant deeds of the father of his country. Here too, a small band of un-dismayed Virginians signalised their valour, checked the triumphant savage, and rescued from total annihilation the dispersed and crest-fallen remnants of those proud battalions, who affected to look down upon them, a few hours before, with all the vaunting arrogance of mili-tary pride. " Braddock's Field," for so the battle ground is called, is now a large farm, owned and cultivated by an individual. The scene of action was on the banks of the river, on an undulating surface, covered at that time with thick woods, but now occupied by enclosed fields. The husbandman now whistles over the consecrated ground, as he toils among the ashes of the brave. Vast quantities of bones have been thrown up by the plough, and at times gathered into heaps and burned ; but a great number still remain, scattered around for the distance of about a mile. These fragments were sufficiently numerous when I last visited this spot, to have designated it as a battle-ground, even to a casual observer who had not been previously aware of the fact.

But the prospect which the good people of Pittsburgh consider as most lovely, "to soul and to eye," is to be found on the northern face of Coal-hill. The yawning caverns which here display their hideous mouths, would have been celebrated among the ancients as the abodes of unpropitious deities; the less classical citizens have peopled them with spirits of sterner stuff—have made them mines of inexhaustible wealth, and drawn from them the materials of substantial comfort. Not only this hill, but the whole of the surrounding country, is full of coal of excellent quality, which is found in immense *strata*, lying almost invariably upon one and the same level. It contains a large proportion of sulphur, and is hard, heavy, and of a deep shining black colour; it is easily ignited, and produces an intense heat; but is very dirty, emits immense volumes of smoke, and throws up an unusual quantity of cinders and dust. These latter fill the atmosphere, and are continually falling in showers, to the great terror of strangers and sojourners, and with manifest injury to the dresses of the ladies, and the white hands of eastern gentlemen. From

this cause, every thing in Pittsburgh wears a
sombre hue; even the snow as it falls brings
with it particles of cinder, and loses its purity
by the connexion. But the people are now so
used to the black and midnight appearance of
objects in their city, as scarcely to be aware
of its inconvenience; so that I once heard a
lady exclaim, on witnessing a snow storm *out
of town,* " La! what *white snow* !"

A disease was formerly prevalent here, which
was attributed to the influence of the coal
smoke. This was a swelling of the glands of
the neck, which produced no pain, nor ultimate
injury, but was an unsightly and incurable
deformity. It was thought to resemble the
goitre, to which the inhabitants of some of the
mountainous parts of Europe are subject. No
case of it has originated for several years; it
is now scarcely to be met with, and is only
found in persons over the middle age, who
contracted it long since. It was therefore
probably owing to some peculiarity in the climate, which has been long since removed
But I am keeping you too long on Coal-hill,
which I will despatch with the remark, that

its summit commands a remarkably fine view
of the city, which is seen from a dizzy height,
lying beneath the spectators' feet, enveloped in
its eternal veil of smoke, which, by rendering
the objects less distinct, seems to throw them
to a greater distance.

It would be an endless task to point out all
the fairy spots with which nature has embellished this romantic country. They who would
court inspiration from the valley or the grove,
or who would prove

" The soft magic of streamlet and hill,"

could scarcely go amiss in the environs of
Pittsburgh. Those hills, those vallies, and
those streams, delight not merely by their intrinsic beauty ; they are endeared to the Pennsylvanian by many fond recollections. The
events which have rendered Fort Pitt and
Braddock's Field conspicuous in history, are
already imprinted upon the mind of every
American ; but every neighbouring eminence
and winding glade has also been the scene of
hardy achievement. This was one of the first

points selected by those who commenced the work of civilization in the western country. Here all the difficulties of a new settlement—the horrors of Indian warfare, and the bereavements of an isolated society, cut off from assistance and almost from intercourse—were encountered to the fullest extent. The Allegheny ridge then presented a formidable barrier, and they who passed it found themselves in a new world, where they must defend themselves or perish ; it was the Rubicon of the adventurous *pioneer.* The first settlers, therefore, waged continual war ; they fought—*pro aris et focis*— for life and all that makes life dear. But these wars were distinguished only by acts of individual prowess ; and produced none of those great events which affect national fame or greatness, and which it is the province of the historian to record. They will therefore find no place in the annals of our country. Yet the day will surely arrive, when the poet and the novelist will traverse these regions in quest of legendary lore, will listen with eagerness to the tales of hoary-headed sires, and laboriously glean the frail and mutilated memorial of the

daring of other days. Then will the gallant
men who smoothed our path, and conquered
for us the country of which we are so proud,
find a place, if not with better men, at least
with the Rodericks and Rob Roys of fiction.

It would require more room than I can
afford, and more patience than I possess, to
give you a detailed account of all the branches of
commerce and manufactures which contribute
to the prosperity of Pittsburgh. The latter
have flourished here extensively, in consequence
of the variety of raw materials indigenous to
the country, the abundance of fuel, the salu-
brity of the climate, the cheapness of provisions,
the convenience of the markets, and the enterprising spirit of the people. The most important branch includes articles manufactured of
iron, a metal which is found in great abundance
in the neighbouring mountains, whence it is
brought in *pigs* and *bars* to this place, at a
small expense, and here wrought for exporta-
tion. Most of the machinery for this and
other purposes is propelled by steam, the
management of which has been brought to
great perfection; but the neighbourhood also

affords many fine water-courses, some of which
are occupied ; cannon, of a very superior quality, have been cast here for the United States'
Service. The manufacture of glass, which was
introduced by the late General O'Hara, about
the year 1798, has been carried on with great success ; there are now a number of establishments
in operation, which produce large quantities of
window-glass, and other ware of the coarser
sort, and one, at which flint glass is made and
ornamented with great elegance. Messrs.
Bakewell, Page, and Bakewell, have the credit
of having introduced the latter branch of this
manufacture ; and their warehouse presents an
endless variety of beautiful ware, designed and
executed in a style which is highly creditable
to their taste and perseverance. Manufactories
of wool and cotton have been supported with
some spirit, but, as yet, with little success.
We have a foolish pride about us, which makes
our gentlemen ashamed of wearing a coat which
has not crossed the Atlantic ; I hope we shall
grow wiser as we grow older. Articles of tin
and leather are fabricated at Pittsburgh to an
astonishing amount. So long ago as 1809,

boots and shoes were manufactured to the amount of seventy thousand dollars; saddlery to the amount of forty thousand, and tin ware to the amount of twenty-five thousand dollars, in one year. In the same year, hats were made to the amount of twenty-five thousand dollars, and cabinet ware to the amount of seventeen thousand. In addition to these, there have been tan-yards, rope-walks, manufactories of white lead and paper, and extensive ship-yards.* You will perceive that I have made this enumeration from data collected several years ago; the increase of population and business has been great, since that time; and when I add, that in addition to the branches already mentioned, all the other mechanic arts receive a proportionable share of attention; it will be seen, that as a manufacturing town, Pittsburgh stands in the first rank, and her rapid rise and progress may be adduced as a proud testimony of American enterprise.

The commerce and trade of Pittsburgh arise

* Nor should I forget some half dozen printing offices and several book-stores, which have been instrumental in consuming a vast deal of ink and paper.

partly from her manufactories, and partly from having long been the place of deposit for goods destined for the western country ; all of which, until very recently, passed from the Atlantic cities, through this place, to their respective points of destination. They are brought in waggons, carrying from thirty-five to fifty hundred pounds each, and embarked at this place in boats. Upwards of four thousand waggon loads of merchandize have been known to enter Pittsburgh in the course of one year, by the main road from Philadelphia alone, in which is not included the baggage and furniture of travellers and emigrants, nor is notice taken of arrivals by other routes. This business has brought an immense quantity of money into circulation at Pittsburgh ; but it has lately been much injured by the competition of Wheeling, and the introduction of steam-boats upon the Ohio. The wealth of this place, however, and its local advantages, must long sustain it against all opposition ; and if the capital of her citizens should eventually be drawn from any branch of commerce, it will probably be thrown into the manufactories, where the profits will be as

great, and much more permanent. Some of
the finest steam-boats which navigate the Ohio,
the James Ross, the General Neville, and many
others, were built here.

This is also a *port of entry,* and here—even
here, at the source of the Ohio—have ships been
built, laden, and cleared out, for the distant
ports of Europe. A curious incident connected
with this subject was mentioned by Mr. Clay
on the floor of Congress. " To illustrate the
commercial habits and enterprise of the American people, (he said) he would relate an
anecdote of a vessel, built, and cleared out at
Pittsburgh for Leghorn. When she arrived at
her place of destination, the master presented
his papers to the custom-house officer, who
would not credit them, and said to him, ' Sir,
your papers are forged ; there is no such port
as Pittsburgh in the world ; your vessel must
be confiscated.' The trembling captain laid
before the officer the map of the United States—
directed him to the gulf of Mexico—pointed
out the mouth of the Mississippi—led him a
thousand miles up it to the mouth of the Ohio,
and thence another thousand up to Pittsburgh.

'There, Sir, is the port whence my vessel cleared out.' The astonished officer, before he had seen the map, would as readily have believed that this vessel had been navigated from the moon."

Of the society I have but little to say, for that is entirely a matter of taste. Strangers are generally pleased with it, for if they do not find, among the male inhabitants, that polished urbanity which distinguishes many of the small towns of the south and west, they are amply repaid for the absence of it by the sweetness and affability of its female denizens, among whom there is a sufficiency of beauty and grace to decorate a ball-room to great advantage. Indeed, I have seldom beheld finer displays of female loveliness than I have witnessed here. There is a small theatre, occasionally occupied by strollers, but often destined to exhibit the histrionic genius of the young gentlemen of the place, among whom the enacting of plays was formerly a fashionable amusement. On such occasions the *dramatis personæ* were represented by a select company, regularly organized, among whom were some beardless youths who personated the females. In this manner some fine displays of genius have been elicited ; the ladies smiled graciously on the enterprise, and the whole was conducted with great decorum.

A seminary of learning has been founded at the town of Allegheny, called the " Western University," and liberally endowed with land by the State Legislature ; but it is not yet organized. An academy in Pittsburgh has heretofore presented the means of classical education, and a number of minor schools have been supported, among which may be mentioned the Sabbath schools, conducted with great spirit and benevolence, by a society composed of the religious of different denominations. There has been also an admirable school for young ladies, and a library company has been established here.

To discipline the body as well as the mind, another institution has been established under the name of the " Western Penitentiary." The stupendous building intended for this purpose is nearly completed, and will form a splendid and commodious edifice. It is situated on an extensive plain, in the town of Allegheny, where this noble pile, with its massy walls and gothic towers, will shew to great advantage.

Twenty years ago, when this settlement was young and insulated, and the savage yet prowled in its vicinity, legal science flourished with a vigour unusual in rude societies. The bench and bar exhibited a galaxy of eloquence and learning.

Judge Addison, who first presided in this circuit, under the present system, possessed a fine mind and great attainments. He was an accomplished scholar, deeply versed in every branch of classical learning. In law and theology he was great ; but although he explored the depths of science with unwearied assiduity, he could sport in the sun-beams of literature, and cull with nice discrimination the flowers of poesy. He assumed his judicial authority under many perplexing circumstances. The country was new, and the people factious ; the bar was undisciplined, and the rules of practice vague ; the judicial system had been newly modelled, and was now to be tested, its excellencies proved, and its defects discovered— and while an unusual weight of responsibility

thus devolved upon the judge, the novelty of
his situation must often have left him without
precedents to govern his decisions. These appalling circumstances would have daunted a
man of less firmness than Judge Addison ; but
his mind possessed an energetic vigour, which
opposition could not subdue, nor difficulty em-
barrass. He pursued a dignified course, which
was equally serviceable to the country and
honourable to himself ; his decisions were so
uniformly correct, that few of them have been
reversed ; they have been published, together
with a number of charges delivered to grand
juries, and the volume is in high repute among
the lawyers of Pennsylvania. I should be happy
to be able to add that this distinguished man
was rewarded for his services, and permitted
to be useful as long as he continued to be
honoured. But it was not so ; he became obnoxious to a dominant faction ; was impeached,
condemned, and hurled from a seat to which
he had given dignity, for an act which was
probably right, but which, if wrong, was not
dishonourable nor corrupt. Such are the effects
of party spirit ; its venom, like a poisonous

miasm, pervades the whole atmosphere in which it is generated, and creates a pestilence, which sweeps worth and worthlessness to a common grave.

This gentleman was succeeded by Judge Roberts, an excellent lawyer, and a man of great integrity and benevolence, who wanted only the energy of his predecessor. He had firmness enough to be always upright; nor could he be swayed from an honest conviction, or intimidated in the discharge of the duties of his office; but he was too mild to enforce a rigid discipline in his court, and too passive for the dispatch of business. He could neither be biassed nor alarmed; but he had too much of the "milk of human kindness" in his nature, and loved mankind too well, to be a judge of men. The hall of justice brings together all the elements of discord; the angry passions are roused; turbulent spirits are brought into contact—life, fortune, and character are at stake— ambition and avarice are busy—hopes and fears are awakened—crime, folly, and misfortune are disclosed—the veil of secrecy is torn from the sorrows of the heart and the scenes of the fire-

side ; and the man who can gaze on such a
scene with a steady eye, controul its every
motion with a firm hand, and decide with
collected promptness, must have a very firm or a
very cold heart. The gentleman of whom I am
speaking had no cold-heartedness in his composition ; his sympathies were easily awakened,
and his was a breast of too much candour and
generosity, to conceal, or be ashamed of, an
honourable impulse. Yet his mind possessed
great vigour and clearness, and he was universally esteemed, as well for his good sense
and attainments, as for his uprightness and
amiability. They who knew him best, will
always remember him with kindness, and his
decisions will be respected when none of us
shall remain who knew his virtues. He died a
few years ago.

Judge Wilkins, who succeeded to this district,
has long been a prominent man. As an advocate, he was among the foremost—distinguished
for his graceful and easy style of speaking, and
his acuteness in the development of testimony ;
and as a citizen he has always been conspicuous. His public spirit, and capacity for

business, have thrown him into a multitude of offices. He presided for many years over one of the branches of the corporation : has represented his country in the Legislature, was President of the Pittsburgh Bank, and of several companies instituted for the purpose of internal improvement. Judge Wilkins brought to the bench an active mind, much legal experience, and an intimate knowledge of the practice of the court over which he presides ; but as he is still on the stage, I must not be his biographer.

There were at the bar in the olden time many illustrious pillars of the law—Steele Semple, long since deceased, a man of stupendous genius, spoken of by his contemporaries as a prodigy of eloquence and legal attainment— James Ross, who is still on the stage, and very generally known as a great statesman and an eminent advocate, who, for depth of thought, beauty of language, melody of voice, and dignity of manners has few equals—Breckenridge, the eccentric, highly gifted Breckenridge, the author of " Modern Chivalry," celebrated for his wit, his singular habits, his frolicksome propensities, and strange adventures, and who

though a successful advocate, and an able
judge, cracked his jokes at the bar, and on the
bench of the supreme court, as freely as at his
own fireside—Woods, Collins, Campbell, and
Mountain, who would have shone at any bar—
Henry Baldwin, an eminent lawyer, a rough,
but powerful and acute speaker, who has lately
been conspicuous in Congress, as chairman of
the committee on domestic manufactures, and
as the author and able advocate of the celebrated
Tariff Bill, with others, whose history has
not reached me. This constellation of wit
and learning, illumining a dusky hemisphere,
presented a singular contrast to the wild and
untutored spirits around them, and the collision
of such opposite characters, together with the
unsettled state of the country, produced a mass
of curious incidents, many of which are still
preserved, and circulate at the bar in the hours
of forensic leisure.

Thus you may perceive that Pittsburgh,
with her dingy aspect, has some strong and
many enticing traits in her character and
history. Her fate is now in her own hands;
she is young, and there is great room for

improvement. By husbanding her resources, opening and extending her channels of commerce, and fostering the native genius of her sons, she may attain a rank which will leave her but few rivals.

Yours, truly.

LETTER III.

WHEELING, AND THE CUMBERLAND ROAD.

DEAR N.

The promises of friendship, like those of love, are often carelessly made, and lightly broken. We are ready to concede any thing to the entreaty of one we love, without reflecting how many little contingencies may interfere with the engagement. Our hearts are indeed but bad economists, and are apt to make liberal promises, which we have neither the ability nor the inclination to fulfil. Thus it is that the last request of a friend, which at parting vibrates feelingly on the ear, and entwines itself among our warmest sympathies, is often obliterated by the pains or pleasures of new scenes and novel avocations. My pledge to you, however, was of such a nature as not to be so easily forgotten. Dearly as I love to lounge away the passing hours, I should feel highly culpable could I forget for a moment that you have a claim to part of them; and independently of this incentive, I assure you that the pleasure I shall experience in participating my sentiments with one so able to appreciate them, will more than compensate me for the labour of making up the record. But for these reflections, believe me, my last long epistle would have exhausted my patience, as I dare say it has yours, and I should never have had the temerity to attempt another. But I have promised to write my travels, and you are doomed to read them.

I left Pittsburgh in a keel boat of about forty-five tons burthen, laden with merchandise, and navigated by eight or ten of those " half-horse and half-alligator " gentry, commonly called *Ohio boatmen*, whose coarse drollery, I foresee already, will afford us some amusement. There is a small cabin in the stern of the boat, which is occupied by two females—not high born damsels, nor yet young nor lovely ; one is the wife of a decent shoemaker, the other is

Crispin's maiden sister, and both are verging into the "sear and yellow leaf." I could wish them more attractive, for I already begin to feel romantic, and could find it in my heart to be very gallant; but I fear that after descanting on the silent beauties of nature, or the noisy revels of my male companions, I shall have to confess, that "all the rest is *leather*." My state room is in the bow of the boat, and is formed by leaving a vacancy, large enough for a bed and chair, among the boxes and barrels which encompass me. I have an excellent bedstead, composed of packages and parcels, so disposed as to receive a comfortable mattrass, and here I snore among British goods and domestic manufactures, as composedly as if neither of those articles had ever caused us one moment's angry discussion. The ample surface of a huge box is devoted to the functions of a table, and my fare is drawn from a small store provided by myself, and consisting of such articles as are easy of preparation. Of the culinary department, I cannot speak in high praise. The cook is an Irish lad, who says he is "a cobbler by trade, and a republican by profession," as careless and as frisky as any of his countrymen, and withal as dirty a wight as you shall meet with in a summer day. But the captain declares that "Richards is as willing a soul as ever lived," which I suppose must make amends for all deficiencies. The deck or roof of the boat affords ample room for a promenade ; and there I saunter or recline, to enjoy the varied hues of the forest, now just budding into luxuriance. When tired of this amusement, or when the sun is too high to allow me to continue it, I retire to my *sanctum sanctorum* below, and read a little, sing a little, whistle a little ; and if all that will not fill up the time, I *turn in* and sleep a little. Thus I manage to pass away the hours in the most tedious of all tiresome situations, that of being imprisoned in a boat.

The view of Pittsburgh from the Ohio is exceedingly beautiful. The rivers Allegheny and Monongahela, with their fine bridges, the surrounding hills, the improvements in the rear of the town, and the villages on each side of it, all shew to great advantage.

The river pursues a winding course to Steubenville, presenting nothing worthy of remark,

F.

but its beautiful scenery, which is in the highest degree romantic. From Steubenville, which is a pretty village in Ohio, we pass on, by Charleston in Virginia, to Wheeling in the same state. This latter place, which the Editor of the Pittsburgh Gazette calls " the little town at the foot of the hill," most truly deserved the pleasant appellation he has given to it ; and I no sooner saw it than I subscribed to the correctness of his *coup-d'œil*. The hill is surely the most conspicuous object in the scene. Wheeling has, however, been much talked of ; and as its inhabitants indulge in golden visions with regard to its future greatness, it may not be useless to examine the grounds of their hopes.

Until within a few years, the immense supplies of merchandise which were imported into the western country, were transported from Philadelphia and Baltimore to Pittsburgh, whence they descended the Ohio to their places of destination. This was one of the great sources of the wealth of Pittsburgh, and she might, and ought to have retained it, had it not been for the culpable negligence and want of spirit of her own citizens and those of Philadelphia. The road to Pittsburgh, extending three hundred miles, through one of the richest states in the Union, was as bad as it was possible for any road to be. Crossing a vast range of mountains, it presented to the eye of the dismayed traveller, a series of steeps and precipices equally difficult and dangerous. The vast number of heavy laden waggons which were daily passing, had worn off the soil which covered the rocks, or converted it into an immense mass of mire. Ravines and gullies intersected the path, which frequently wound along the very verge of hideous gulfs that yawned to receive the tottering traveller. By this road the western merchant laboriously dragged his freightage to the shores of the Ohio. In vain were remonstrances made and reiterated on this subject. In vain did a few public spirited individuals appeal to the justice and generosity of Pennsylvania—in vain did they address her interest and her honour. The Pennsylvanians affected to despise the trade of the western country as a matter of little importance ; but, in fact, they neglected to secure it because they imagined it to be already secure. They believed that the western traders could purchase goods to advantage *only* at Philadelphia, and that they could transport them to the Ohio by *no other* route than that leading through Pittsburgh. The inference from this sort of reasoning was, that it would be time enough to make a good road through their state a half century hence, when they should have grown rich enough to expend money on such *luxuries;* and that in the meanwhile the western people must drag their merchandize over rocks and mountains, and through mud and water, the best way they could. But the western people were by no means satisfied with such treatment. In their annual excursions to the eastward, they expended hundreds of thousands of dollars in Pennsylvania, and they thought it but fair that the people whom they had thus enriched should take some pains to render the trade as convenient and advantageous as possible to all parties. They found that in some seasons they could procure transportation to Pittsburgh at four dollars per hundred pounds, and that at others they were obliged to pay more than double that sum—a disparity occasioned chiefly by the state of the road in good or bad weather. It seemed to follow, as a natural consequence, that if a safe and permanent road was made, the lowest price which they now paid *at any* season would become the average price for *all seasons;* and they conceived all above that to be an unjust tax paid to Pennsylvania. They of course began to cast about in search of a remedy for the evil.

In the meantime, from the causes I have already mentioned, as well as others of a more general nature, serious inquiries began to be made on the subject of connecting the eastern and western sections of the Union, by a channel of intercourse more safe and expeditious than those which already existed. Various routes were proposed. The people of the State of New York, with a liberality and promptitude which does them infinite honour, projected, at the instigation of the discerning Clinton, their grand canal from the Hudson to the Lakes, expecting through this channel to become possessed of a large portion of the western trade. That work is nearly finished; and while it can-

not fail to prove a rich and lasting source of
prosperity to New York, it will immortalize the
name of that illustrious patriot, who has devoted
for years the whole energy of his fertile genius
to its accomplishment.

The western representation in Congress, on
the other hand, headed by Mr. Clay, devised the
National Turnpike, or, as it is commonly called,
the Cumberland Road. This project was proposed in such a form as to meet the approbation
of the Executive, who, pleased with the idea of
strengthening the bonds of the Federal Union,
by facilitating the intercourse between its two
grand divisions, easily came into the plan of
establishing a great permanent route, which
should lead from the metropolis through the
western states.   Thus supported, a law was
passed, making an appropriation for a section
of the road, to extend from Cumberland
(formerly Fort Cumberland), in Maryland, to
Wheeling, in Virginia.   This section of the
road, which embraces the Allegheny mountains, has since been completed, in a manner
which reflects the highest credit upon those
engaged in its construction.   It is a permanent

turnpike, built of stone, and covered with gravel, so as to unite solidity and smoothness; and noble arches of stone have been thrown, at a vast expense, over all the ravines and water-courses. In some places the road is hewn into the precipitous side of the mountain, and the traveller, beholding a vast abyss beneath his feet, while the tall cliffs rising to the clouds overhang his path, is struck with admiration at the bold genius which devised, and the persevering hardihood which executed, so great a work. Those frightful precipices, which once almost defied the approach of the nimble footed hunter, are now traversed by heavy laden waggons; and pleasure carriages roll rapidly along where beasts of prey but lately found a secure retreat. Another appropriation has since been made to extend this road to Zanesville in Ohio; and commissioners have been appointed to survey and trace out its route to the shores of the Mississippi. The right of the government to make these appropriations, has been warmly contested on the floor of Congress, and has elicited some of the finest displays of talent which have ever emanated from that distinguished body. Mr. Clay, who could never brook the inaction of the Speaker's chair, when an important question animated the august assembly over which he presided, exhibited some of the happiest efforts of his eloquence in this important but apparently dry discussion, and, by his successful exertions, added another to the many benefits conferred on his fellow-citizens by the accomplished orator of the west.

Cumberland is a pretty little town, delightfully situated on a branch of the Potomac, and in one of those romantic spots which are often found in mountainous and secluded situations. Braddock assembled his army here, at the commencement of the celebrated campaign which ended in his defeat and death; and he passed the mountains by nearly the same route which has been selected for the national road. This path was traced by an Indian guide, who, with that instinctive acuteness for which the whole race is remarkable, added, no doubt, to an intimate knowledge of the country, at once

struck out the very course which the experience of half a century has proved to be the
best and shortest.

The Pennsylvanians were at last roused from
their apathy by the successful exertions which
they saw in operation to the north and south
of them to divert the western trade into new
channels. To do them justice, they had
expended a great deal of money upon the
Pittsburgh road; but it had been appropriated
in small sums, and much of it injudiciously
applied. It ought also, in fairness, to be remarked, that this route, after leaving Cham-
bersburgh, passes in general through a mountainous and sterile region, thinly populated,
and possessing but little wealth; and that the
richest and most populous parts of the state,
lying at a distance from it, had no immediate
interest in a road, which neither brought money
into their neighbourhood, nor extended to them
the conveniences of travelling. A majority
therefore of the legislature anticipated no
benefit to their respective districts from the
application of money to this object, the advantages of which they believed to be confined to

Pittsburgh, Philadelphia, and the intermediate country.

About the year 1817, Mr. Breck, of Philadelphia, at that time in the Pennsylvanian legislature, and more recently a member of Congress, issued a pamphlet, in which he endeavoured to draw the legislative attention to the subject of slack-water navigation. His work is valuable on several grounds—1, as shewing what has already been done for the promotion of internal improvements in his native state, and therein exhibiting many facts highly honourable to her public spirit; 2, as shewing what remains to be done; and, 3, as pointing out the ample resources of the state for executing the works which he recommends, and eloquently advocating an appropriation of them to those purposes. His favourite project seems to be that of uniting the Delaware and Ohio, by means of canals. For this purpose, he proposes to cut a canal from the waters of the Schuylkill to those of the Susquehanna, and from the head waters of the Susquehanna to those of the Allegheny. This part of the work contains many interesting details, useful facts, and

correct inferences ; but, unfortunately, Mr.
Breck with a great deal of practical good sense
mingles some degree of enthusiasm. His notions are entirely too speculative for common
use. He carries us over mountains, or round
them, with a facility that surprises us. Rocks
and precipices present no obstacle to his enterprising genius. We accompany him with
great pleasure, and even without suspicion,
until we get to the end of the journey ;
but then we look back and wonder how
we get there. He seems equally surprised
at his own success ; for, on arriving at Pittsburgh, he is so much elated that nothing
short of the Pacific Ocean bounds his prospects. He carries us down the Ohio, and up
the Mississippi ; and, triumphantly ascending
the cliffs of the Rocky Mountains, shews how
easy it would be to unite the waters of the
latter with those of the Columbia ; and exult-
ingly prophesies that the day will come when
our teas and India muslins will be transported
by this route from the Pacific Ocean to Philadelphia. All this *may*, and probably *will*, be
done hereafter, and a proud day for America
will be that which witnesses its accomplish-

ment; but it would be as well for *us* to leave the
question to be discussed in the legislature of
some future state to be *located* among the Rocky
Mountains, or before a Congress which may
be held at St. Louis, or perhaps at Shawnee
Town.—Who knows? Do not suppose that I
mean to jest with Mr. Breck's book. He is a
man highly respected, as well for his genius
as for the excellence of his heart and principles; but the wisest of men in all ages have
had their hobby-horses, and we are assured
from high authority that there is no disputing
against them.

This pamphlet was immediately followed by
another, from the pen of Mr. John E. Howard,
Junior, of Baltimore, a member of the Executive
Council of Maryland. This gentleman publishes
a variety of official reports and other documents,
on the subject of roads and inland navigation,
which afford ample testimony that his own
state has not been backward in her attention to
this important branch of political economy.
He strenuously advocates the policy of con-
tending with Pennsylvania for the western
trade; and shews, by a series of facts and cal-
culations, the practicability of throwing a large

portion, if not the whole of it, into the arms of
Baltimore. His distinct proposition is, to complete a turnpike to intersect the Cumberland
road, by which means a route will be opened
all the way from Baltimore to the Ohio. This
he shews can easily be done, as several sections
of the route which he proposes to pursue have
already been *turnpiked*, either by the state or
by private companies. I cannot give you his
estimate of the expense, as I write from memory entirely; but it is quite inconsiderable.
He combats some of Mr. Breck's notions, with
considerable ability; but at the same time
treats that gentleman with the courtesy which
is due to his genius and patriotism, and, on the
whole, conducts the controversy with a liberal
and gentlemanly spirit.

The next champion who took to the high-
way in this contest, was Mr. Neville, the able
editor of the Pittsburgh Gazette. Hitherto,
the writers on this subject were eastern men,
who, probably, thought more of the interest of
their respective cities than of the western
country. It was gratifying, therefore, to see
the question taken up by a gentleman of ac-

knowledged abilities, on this side of the mountains, and conspicuous for his attachment to
western interests.   He at once defeats Mr.
Breck's canal project, by stating the simple
fact, that a canal through the region which
the one alluded to is proposed to pass, would
be *frozen up* four months in the year, and that
in the summer season some of the streams
proposed to be navigated would not contain
water enough to float a canoe—the Juniata, for
instance.   He urges, with much eloquence, the
more reasonable and feasible plan of completing
the Philadelphia road, and clearing the bed of
the Ohio from Pittsburgh to Wheeling.   He
states the fact, upon the authority of experienced
boatmen, that the impediments of the Ohio
between Pittsburgh and Wheeling are not
greater than between Wheeling and Maysville,
and that there is no season when boats may
descend from Wheeling in which they cannot
descend also from Pittsburgh.   Mr. Neville,
therefore, seems to consider the competition of
Wheeling to be by no means formidable, and
contends that the western trade may still be
kept in the old channel, if the people of Penn-

sylvania can be brought to see their own interests, and to exercise their energies with that enterprise and liberality which the occasion so loudly demands. This writer adverts with much feeling to the neglected situation of the Ohio. That noble stream, which is useless to us during the summer months, may be so improved by removing the obstructions in its channel, as to be navigable at all seasons. At the very time that Mr. Neville was engaged in this argument, the existence of a single fact proved the correctness of his views. There was at that time (in the autumn of 1818) merchandize worth *three millions of dollars*, belonging to the western merchants, lying along the shores of the Monongahela, waiting a rise of water to convey them to their places of destination. The western merchants were lounging discontentedly about the streets of Pittsburgh, or moping idly in its taverns, like the victims of an ague. From these, and a variety of other facts, our author felt himself authorised to call on the State to rise in the majesty of its power, to preserve a lucrative and important trade from being diverted into foreign channels.

The treasury of Pennsylvania is not only
solvent, but in a flourishing condition, and the
credit of that state has always stood so high
that she is able to command, at any time, the
most ample resources.   Philadelphia, by the
wealth, steady habits, and extensive credit
abroad of her merchants, has it in her power
to furnish the traders of the west with better
assortments of goods, and those at lower prices,
than can yet be afforded by Baltimore.   But
Baltimore is not a rival to be despised : though
young, she is public spirited ; her citizens are
acute and enterprising ; when excited, they are
full of fire : and though that fire has sometimes
kindled a conflagration in her own bosom, it must
be irresistible when properly directed.   If the
Pennsylvanians, therefore, neglect to cherish
the trade which has poured millions of dollars
into the state, Philadelphia and Pittsburgh will
be forsaken ; Baltimore will become the mart,
and Wheeling the place of deposit.   The situation of the latter place is pretty enough, except
that the hill at the foot of which the town is built
is so near to the river as to leave but little
room for its expansion.   Some buildings, how-

ever, have been erected on a flat, a little lower
down. An eminence, at the back of the town,
over which the turnpike passes, affords one of
the finest prospects imaginable; the place is
healthy, the inhabitants respectable and correct in their dealings, and the society good.

It is not, perhaps, a matter of great importance to the western people whether they
purchase their goods at Philadelphia or at
Baltimore, or whether they transport them by
way of Pittsburgh or of Wheeling. Time will
decide these rival claims; the western merchant will make his purchases where he can do
it to most advantage, and will transport his
goods by the cheapest and most expeditious
route. The establishment of steam-boats has
carried much of this trade to New Orleans; but
how far this place will ultimately interfere with
the eastern cities I must examine hereafter.

I have noticed the contest between rival
states and cities, not to claim the palm of superior enterprise for either, but to pourtray the
progress of a noble emulation, of which the
results have been beneficial to all the parties
concerned, and highly honourable to our com-

F

mon country. New York, Pennsylvania, and
Maryland, have marched singly to their respective objects; the two latter have completed
their roads, and the latter will soon exhibit to
an admiring world, the most extensive and important chain of artificial inland navigation
ever witnessed. The patriotic state of Virginia
has opened her eyes to this interesting subject,
and is treading on the heels of her more commercial sisters. The beautiful Potomac, whose
picturesque shores have heretofore been only
trod by the curious traveller, is now traced by
the eager feet of science; and those precipitous
currents whose wild beauty warmed the sage
of Monticello to rapture, are about to be converted to the useful purposes of commerce.
The Chesapeake and Delaware are also about
to be united by canals; and these works tend
directly to facilitate the desired intercourse
between the shores of the Atlantic and those
of the Mississippi.

But there are other points of view in which
this subject is highly interesting. By the controversy to which I have alluded, together with
the writings of Governor Clinton, of New York,

Mr. William J. Duane, of Philadelphia, and others, it appears that the spirit of improvement is awakened in various sections of our country, and that men distinguished by their popularity, abilities, and official rank, conceive it worthy of their notice. It seems also that the rising greatness of the western country is not unnoticed, nor the value of her commerce disregarded.

It shews further that she has more than one outlet for her produce. Mr. Cobbett, who, with all his disaffection towards his own country, is a true Englishman in his hatred of all that is estimable in ours, inquires, in his letters to Mr. Birkbeck, " in case of a war with England, what would become of your market *down the Mississippi ?* That is your *sole market.* That way your produce *must go ;* or you must dress yourselves in skins, and tear your food to bits with your hands." " On this side of the mountains there are twelve hundred miles of coast to blockade ; but you gentlemen prairie owners are like the rat that has but one hole to go out and come in at." Observations of this kind, evincing a deplorable ignorance of the country and its resources, it is easy to answer. Every distinct proposition in these quotations is untrue. In the first place we doubt, to use the mildest language, whether England will ever have it in her power again to blockade an American port; but leaving that point to be settled by our gallant navy, we answer that we are under no compulsion to carry our produce down the Mississippi, nor are we dependent on any foreign country for the conveniences of life. A very large portion of the western people manufacture their own clothing; among the farmers the practice is universal : and it extends so far to other classes that it is not at all unusual to see professional gentlemen in affluent circumstances, and men of high official rank, clad in plain domestic fabrics. I could name several of our most distinguished public characters, who make it a rule to wear no cloth which is not manufactured in their own families; and in the event of such a war as is anticipated for us, that patriotism which has always distinguished the American ladies would glow with its wonted energy, and the world would soon learn that their ingenuity is equal to their scorn of

dependence.   We have food, and the means of
preparing it.   The perfection to which the manufacture of cutlery, and various articles of
steel and iron, has been brought in the United
States, leaves us no cause to dread our being
ever obliged to substitute our *fingers* for forks.
Is it so soon forgotten that the cutlasses of our
gallant tars, and the bayonets of our patriotic
soldiers, which during the late war, triumphed
over the boasted invincibility of *British steel*,
were, like the hands that wielded them, of domestic origin?   Shall we fear that our firesides
will be visited by want, while the same inventive genius exists which devised the means of
repelling the invader from our shores?   Or is
it meant to be insinuated, that it is easier to
supply weapons for the capture of British frigates, than utensils for the purposes of domestic economy?

As to the outlet for our produce, we say, admitting Mr. Cobbett's premises, that, if we cannot descend the Mississippi, we can ascend the
Ohio.   It is a well known fact, that large
quantities of fur and peltry, have been carried
from St. Louis to Philadelphia, by way of

Pittsburgh; and that the saltpetre, tobacco, and hempen yarn of Kentucky have been carried to the same market, by the same route. Such was the destination of a large portion of the produce of the west, before the late war, when the Mississippi was open, and when the formidable obstructions to the passage of the Allegheny mountains, which I have noticed above, existed to their fullest extent. When our coasting trade was interrupted by the war, all the western produce, except that destined for consumption at New Orleans, necessarily ascended the Ohio; and large quantities of sugar, coffee, and other heavy merchandise, were transported from New Orleans to Philadelphia, by the same inland route. Even yet a large portion of the bacon and venison hams of Kentucky, are sold at Pittsburgh. Lately, the introduction of steam-boats has carried most of this produce down the river; but if, when the Mississippi was open, any portion of the produce of the west has been transported up the Ohio, what would be done if the navigation of the former should be closed? Surely the inference is plain, that if produce could be shipped up the Ohio, with advantage, when no obstacle existed at the mouth of the Mississippi, there could be no great hardship in forcing it into the same channel, when that river should be closed. It may also be added, that, until lately, merchandise was conveyed in small boats, slowly and laboriously propelled against the powerful current of the Ohio, by human labour, while it is now cheaply and expeditiously transported by the agency of steam. Large steam-boats now ascend the river as far as Pittsburgh, in high water; but in the event alluded to, our streams would be covered with lighter vessels, propelled by steam, which would bid defiance to every obstacle, except the shoals created by low water, in dry seasons, and as this obstacle now exists, and impedes the descending, as much as ascending navigation, we should be no worse off in that respect than we are at present. Even those temporary obstacles it is supposed will be soon removed. The States of Pennsylvania, Virginia, Ohio, and Kentucky, united a few years since in the appointment of commissioners to survey the bed of the Ohio, and report the facts, with their opinion as to the practicability of improving its navigation. After a careful examination they made a report, which justified the hope that this work would not be long delayed. Since that time Congress has made a liberal appropriation towards executing this desirable object. Major Long, an officer of the Engineers, of high reputation, was directed two years ago, to commence the work, by making experiments upon six of the sandbanks in the Ohio; and should he succeed in devising a successful plan for their removal, it is expected that the work will be extended throughout the whole course of this noble river. He commenced last year, and proceeded with flattering prospects, until his operations were suspended by the rising of the water; his labours will be resumed when the river shall again have fallen.

The country also presents ample natural advantages for opening other channels of trade. The State of Ohio, part of which borders on Lake Erie, will be intersected with roads and canals, as soon as the people of New York shall have completed their great work. A canal from the waters of the Miami to those of Lake Erie has been already commenced, with so vigorous a spirit, and such ample means, as enable us to cherish the proud hope of its speedy accomplishment. The legislature of Illinois have caused a survey of the country between the navigable waters of the Illinois river, and Lake Michigan, to be made by able engineers, who report that this communication may be opened at an expense of about seven hundred thousand dollars. A canal company has since been incorporated, and thus a commencement has been made in this important design, which when effected will open a water communication from the States of Illinois and Missouri, to the city of New York.

As I have spoken of the public spirit of Pennsylvania, and particularly of her two principal cities, allow me to explain myself on that subject. I am far from wishing to derogate from the honour of my native state. The merchants and gentlemen of Philadelphia are liberal and high minded men; but they are in the habit of attending more to *their own,* and less to *public* business, than the same class of society in almost any other part of the United States. They have a regular routine of avocation, which they seldom allow to be broken in upon, by affairs which are not of immediate interest; consequently they are less intimately acquainted with the character, and resources of their own state, than gentlemen of other cities; much less so than could be expected from men so well educated, and so enlightened on other subjects. Many of the most intelligent persons in Philadelphia are utterly ignorant of the geography, population, improvements, and productions of the interior and western parts of the state. Men who can converse learnedly of the classics, and tastefully of the fine arts, who are intimately acquainted with European history, politics, and manners, and who scrutinize with critical acuteness the measures of the federal government, glance with careless, uninquiring eyes at the lofty mountains, and fertile vallies, within the bounds of their own commonwealth. They of course feel little interest in subjects upon which they think so little.

The state of politics too, in Pennsylvania, has had much influence in preventing the growth of public spirit. *Party spirit* has raged in that devoted land, with ungovernable fury; the bitterness of contention has been permitted to inflame and corrode the public mind; the gall of political enmity has been infused into the cup of social intercourse, and the interests of the state have been too often forgotten, in the tumult of schemes to raise or to defeat a party, to prostrate or to exalt an individual. These contests have been distinguished by a virulence hardly known elsewhere, and a scurrilous personality which could no where else be tolerated. Men of feeling and modesty shrink from such conflicts; however willing they might be to bare their breasts in honourable war, they covet not the odious distinction of exposing their reputations as targets for the archery of faction. No men would be more apt to stand aloof on such occasions than the Philadelphians, reared as they are, in the practice of temperance, and in habits of chaste methodical reflection. The state is consequently deprived of the use of much talent which she certainly possesses. Do not understand me as making any comparison between the dominant party, and the minority. My position is simply this, that

where party spirit is carried to such excess as
to alienate friends, and distract society, so that
men look with jaundiced eyes upon each other,
the arm of government must be paralysed, and
the impulses of patriotism benumbed. The
man who possesses the genius to devise, or the
wealth to execute, will not co-operate with him
whose popularity enables him to gain the voice
of the people, or the sanction of the ruling
powers. When a work, however noble, which
is proposed by one party, is sure to be de-
nounced by the other, men of talent retire from
the disgusting controversy, and the wealthy
refuse to risk their gold in uncertain and contested schemes, generated in the storms of faction, and crushed by its whirlwinds.

Yet when, in spite of all these obstacles, we
observe what Pennsylvania has accomplished :
when we see the fine bridges over the Delaware, the Schuylkill, the Susquehanna, the
Allegheny, and the Monongahela; the noble
turnpike roads in the eastern part of the state ;
the splendid public buildings in Philadelphia,
her charitable institutions, and her literary
monuments ; we cannot but acknowledge, that

she *has* the *spirit*, nor refrain from deploring the existence of those counteracting causes which restrain its exercise. The Fair Mount water-works alone, must rescue Philadelphia from the charge of a penurious or timid policy, where her own interests are immediately concerned. But more expanded views, and more liberal exertions, are expected from her wealth and her intelligence. The trade of the western country is destined to become more important than the commerce of the Atlantic ; and this she must secure by liberal expenditures, or yield it to her rivals.

LETTER IV.

SCENERY OF THE OHIO—DROLLERIES OF
THE BOATMEN—RIVER MELODIES.

April 18th. Between Wheeling and Marietta, there is little worthy of the traveller's
attention, except the mounds and fortifications
on Mr. Tomlinson's farm at Grave Creek.
The " Big Grave," as it is called, is about a
quarter of a mile from Mr. Tomlinson's house,
in a south-westerly direction; it is a circular
mound, sixty-eight feet high, and fifty-five feet
in diameter at the summit. This is one of
the largest mounds in the Western country,
and exhibits every indication of great antiquity,
its whole surface being covered with forest
trees of the largest size, and the earth presenting no peculiarity to distinguish it from the
adjacent soil.

The "Long Reach," where the Ohio pursues a direct course for seventeen miles, may also be noticed in this place, as presenting a remarkable exception to the general character of this river.

19th. Marietta is beautifully situated at the mouth of the Muskingum river, and has an appearance of neatness and regularity, which is not usual in the villages of the country. Ship-building was carried on here, to some extent, several years ago : and great expectations were formed as to the future commercial importance of the town, which have as yet been but partially realized. As early as the year 1798 or 99 Commodore Preble built a brig of one hundred and twenty tons at this place, which probably was the first sea vessel launched in the western waters.

I would gladly have stopped for a short time at this place, for I began to be heartily tired of the boat. A voyage of any kind is disagreeable enough, at best: for, give it what variety you may, it still involves confinement of the body, and a correspondent restraint of the mind. The muses, indeed, have sometimes

condescended to visit the prisoner in his cell ;
like charitable damsels, they have hovered
round the bed of sickness, and by their magic
spells, have chased away the pangs of sorrow
and disease. Even when disconcerted love
makes his exit at the window, the generous
Nine remain to cheer the son of penury, illu-
minating his dreary abode with their brightest
illusions. But I have not heard of their deign-
ing to honour a keel-boat with their presence ;
and, with reverence be it spoken, it would, in
spite of the maids of Helicon, be but a sad
prison-house after all. The fancy, it is true,
might wander over boundless regions, but the
feet are as fond of wandering as the imagination, and it is by no means pleasant to have
them confined to entire inaction, or limited
within the space of a few yards. Yet disagreeable as such a situation naturally is, I have
found so many recreations to amuse me on the
present occasion, so much novelty in the objects which are continually presented, and so
much interest in the recollections which crowd
upon my mind, that I cannot say my most idle
moments have been burdensome ; and I am

convinced that, with the aid of a little ingenuity, and some good humour, no man need
ever despair.

The heart must indeed be cold that would
not glow among scenes like these. Rightly
did the French call this stream *La Belle Rivière*
(the beautiful river). The sprightly Canadian,
plying his oar in cadence with the wild notes
of the boat-song, could not fail to find his
heart enlivened by the beautiful symmetry of
the Ohio. Its current is always graceful, and
its shores every where romantic. Every thing
here is on a large scale. The eye of the traveller is continually regaled with magnificent
scenes. Here are no pigmy mounds dignified
with the name of mountains, no rivulets
swelled into rivers. Nature has worked with
a rapid but masterly hand; every touch is bold,
and the whole is grand as well as beautiful;
while room is left for art to embellish and
fertilize that which nature has created with
a thousand capabilities. There is much sameness in the character of the scenery; but that
sameness is in itself delightful, as it consists in
the recurrence of noble traits, which are too

G

pleasing ever to be viewed with indifference; like
the regular features which we sometimes find
in the face of a lovely woman, their charm
consists in their own intrinsic gracefulness,
rather than in the variety of their expressions.
The Ohio has not the sprightly, fanciful wildness of the Niagara, the St. Lawrence, or the
Susquehanna, whose impetuous torrents, rushing
over beds of rocks, or dashing against the jutting
cliffs, arrest the ear by their murmurs, and
delight the eye with their eccentric wander-
ings. Neither is it like the Hudson, margined
at one spot by the meadow and the village, and
overhung at another by threatening precipices
and stupendous mountains. It has a wild,
solemn, silent sweetness, peculiar to itself.
The noble stream, clear, smooth, and unruffled,
swept onward with regular majestic force.
Continually changing its course, as it rolls
from vale to vale, it always winds with dignity,
and avoiding those acute angles, which are
observable in less powerful streams, sweeps
round in graceful bends, as if disdaining the
opposition to which nature forces it to submit.
On each side rise the romantic hills, piled on

each other to a tremendous height ; and between them, are deep, abrupt, silent glens,
which at a distance seem inaccessible to the
human foot; while the whole is covered with
timber of a gigantic size, and a luxuriant
foliage of the deepest hues. Throughout this
scene there is a pleasing solitariness, that speaks
peace to the mind, and invites the fancy to
soar abroad, among the tranquil haunts of medi-
tation.   Sometimes the splashing of the oar is
heard, and the boatman's song awakens the
surrounding echoes ; but the most usual music
is that of the native songsters, whose melody
steals pleasingly on the ear, with every modu-
lation, at all hours. and in every change of situation. The poet, in sketching these solitudes,
might, by throwing his scene a few years back,
add the light canoe and war-song of the Indian ;
but the peaceful traveller rejoices in the absence of that which would bring danger as well
as variety within his reach.

These remarks apply to the Ohio, only so
far as I have already seen it; after we leave
this hilly region, its shores no doubt present a
different aspect. We have just passed the

Muskingum Island, and already the country seems to be much less mountainous though not less romantic. The prospect immediately below this island, is singularly picturesque and characteristic. The river, making a long stretch to the west, affords an uninterrupted view for several miles. On one side are seen several log-houses, surrounded by newly cleared fields, exhibiting the first stage of improvement; a little further on, a neat brick-house, with a numerous collection of fruit trees, just putting forth their blossoms, indicate a more advanced state of civilization, and mark the residence of a wealthier or more industrious citizen. Beyond these are lofty hills, whose long shadows fall upon the water, and all around is the gloom of the forest. On the opposite bank, a rude bridge, thrown over a deep ravine, is discovered through the trees; and near it, a few pail inclosures, fabricated of rough stakes, designate and protect the tombs of some of the early adventurers to this wild country.

I never was a friend to the incarceration of beauty, as I always believed that every pretty woman, to say nothing of the ugly ones, was

intended to assist in beguiling the cares of some
poor fellow, who, like myself, had more of them
on his shoulders than he could well attend to.
Yet, whenever I gaze on the silent shores of
the Ohio, I am tempted to think how pretty a
convent would look in one of these romantic
vallies, where deep, melancholy shadows curtain
every spot, where no discordant sound dis-
turbs the solitude, and where no unhallowed
object intrudes upon the eye to excite a " tumult in a vestal's veins." But this illusion is
easily destroyed ; when I forsook the deck, and
strolled into the country among the farmers,
who, fearing the atmosphere of the river, build
their houses at a distance, leaving a strip of
the forest standing to intercept the damps, I
found something very different from nuns and
anchorites.

To-day our boat struck on a sand-bar,
through the carelessness of the captain, who
was asleep in the cabin. The boatmen jumped
into the water with great alacrity, and attempted
to " heave her off;" but being unable to effect
it, we were obliged to procure a flat boat, to
lighten, and hands to assist us. These were

readily and cheerfully furnished in the neighbourhood, and we suffered no other inconvenience than that of a few hours' detention.
In the meanwhile, I took my fowling-piece,
and scoured the forest on the Virginia side of
the river. After shooting some squirrels, which
were very abundant, I stopped at a farm house,
where I was hospitably received. My arrival had
been foretold, not like that of Fitz-James, by a
" minstrel old and gray," but by the good man
of the house, who said he had heard the report of
a *shot gun* in the woods, and knew *there were
strangers about.* He eyed my piece with a good
deal of contempt, and wondered at my using
it in preference to a rifle. Throughout the
west, the fowling-piece is viewed rather as a
toy for children than as a weapon for man.
Hunting is here, as Scot describes it to have
been among the ancient Highlanders,

" Mimicry of noble war."

The people scorn a weapon less deadly than the
rifle, and practice has made them remarkably
expert in the use of this national arm. " Luck's
like a *shot-gun*, mighty uncertain," is a common

saying, and indeed the poor *shot-gun* is a standing but for ridicule, and a common subject of comparison with every thing that is insignificant.

To-day we passed two large rafts lashed together, by which simple conveyance several families from New England were transporting themselves and their property to the land of promise in the western woods. Each raft was eighty or ninety feet long, with a small house erected on it ; and on each was a stack of hay, round which several horses and cows were feeding, while the paraphernalia of a farm-yard, the ploughs, waggons, pigs, children, and poultry, carelessly distributed, gave to the whole more the appearance of a permanent residence, than of a caravan of adventurers seeking a home. A respectable looking old lady, with *spectacles on nose*, was seated on a chair at the door of one of the cabins, employed in knitting ; another female was at the wash-tub ; the men were chewing their tobacco, with as much complacency as if they had been in "the land of steady habits," and the various family avocations seemed to go on like clock-work. In this

manner these people travel at a slight expense.
They bring their own provisions; their raft
floats with the current; and honest Jonathan,
surrounded with his scolding, grunting, squalling,
and neighing dependants, floats to the *point
proposed* without leaving his own fire-side; and
on his arrival there, may step on shore with his
house, and commence business, like a certain
grave personage, who, on his marriage with a
rich widow, said he had " nothing to do but to
walk in and hang up his hat."

The evening of this day brought us to Parkersburgh, a small village in Virginia, famous
for its manufactory of bank notes, of which a
goodly quantity were, some years ago, ushered
into an ephemeral existence. They have now
entirely disappeared—the shop is shut; and as
this species of domestic industry finds no protection in Mr. Baldwin's tariff bill, the inhabitants will be obliged to exert their ingenuity
upon some other branch of the arts. The town,
composed of a few scattered houses, is beautifully situated : the approach by water from
above is singularly pretty, the houses presenting
themselves through a cluster of intervening trees,

which, with a proper taste, have been allowed
to stand on the shore. We had but a glimpse
of it in the twilight, when the lights shining
through the numerous foliage might have reminded one of a Chinese feast of lanterns; and
we were so long in getting to the shore, that
even these were extinguished before we reached
it. The sky was delightfully serene, and the
moon-beams, playing over the tree-tops, and
drawing out the forest-shadows into a thousand fantastic shapes, invited us to a stroll.
Our curiosity was soon satisfied; the villagers
had retired to rest; the silence of the forest was
around their dwellings; the stranger's footsteps
alone disturbed it. We, therefore, soon returned; but the boatmen were more successful
in their researches after novelty. In their little
tour they discovered one of those engines of
justice, to which the philanthropic compiler of
the *Navigator* has devoted a page or two of
invective, namely, a vile whipping-post, mouldering with age, or drooping, perhaps, like many
other faithful public servants, with neglect and
long disuse. The honest old gentleman, last mentioned, could not have been more scandalized

at the appearance of this unsightly fixture, than
were our unenlightened mariners, who were un-
accustomed to this instrument of punishment,
which they forthwith removed from its place,
and launched into the river, observing that
" them that wanted to be whipped *mought* go
after it."

Nor did the amusements of the night end
here. The adventure of the whipping-post had
exhilarated the spirits of the crew, who now
seating themselves in groups upon the bank,
inspired, no doubt, by the genial influence of
the " chaste cold moon," began to chaunt their
rude ditties of " *bold young fellers*" and "ladies
gay," an accomplishment in which some of
them had acquired a tolerable proficiency, and
which they all appeared to value more highly
than their rough natures would seem to indicate. Here was a fund of entertainment for
me. It is amusing to see poetry dressed in
rags and limping upon crutches; dignified and
lovely as she is in her robes of majesty, she
becomes the most quaint, ingenious, entertaining little imp imaginable, when she condescends
to play the hoyden; and I assure you I adored

her with tenfold ardour when I beheld her
versatility, and saw her, like a good republican,
dispensing her smiles, as well upon the lowly
as upon the great. She has, indeed, risen
wonderfully in my opinion—in which of late
years she had rather sunk, in consequence of
the suspicious company she had kept ;—a vi-
rago with Byron, a voluptuary with Moore,
and with Monk Louis a wrinkled old hag.
She has again appeared in her native integrity.
I have seen her in the robes of Nature, and
heard her in the innocency of her heart. To
the admirers of the simplicity of Wordsworth,
to those who prefer the naked effusions of the
heart to the meretricious ornaments of fancy,
I present the following beautiful specimen,
verbatim, as it flowed from the lips of an Ohio
boatman :—

> " It's oh ! as I was a wal-king out,
>   One morning in July,
> I met a maid, who ax'd my trade—
>   Says I, I'll tell you presently,
>   Miss, I'll tell you presently.
>
> And its oh ! she was so neat a maid,
>   That her stockings and her shoes
> She *toted* in her lilly white hands,
>   For to keep them from the dews," &c. &c.

I challenge the admirers of that celebrated poet to point out, in all his works, or in those of his disciples, a single verse, which is as simple, as descriptive, or which contains so much matter in so small a compass, as either of the above.

In the following amatory stanza, the lover betrays his tenderness with great delicacy :—

> " Here's to you, and all the rest,
> And likewise her that I love best ;
> As she's not here to take a part,
> I'll drink her health with all my heart."

What a manly spirit breathes through each line, where the poet pays an honest tribute to poverty ; sympathises with the forlorn wight, too often the object of ridicule, who lives in *single wretchedness ;* and satirises the cupidity of the world, all in the compass of a single stanza ! It runs thus :—

> " Here's to those that has old clothes,
> And never a wife to mend 'em ;
> A plague on those that has halfjoes,
> And has'n't a heart to spend 'em !"

There was one ballad particularly, of a very

pathetic nature, which I regret I have forgotten, as the singer observed, very feelingly, that he " *set more store to it*" than to all the rest. It began thus :—

> " Oh ! its love was the 'casion of my downfall,
> I wish I had'n't never lov'd none at all !
> Oh ! its love was the 'casion of my mis*eree ;*
> Now I am bound, but once I was free !"

The following exquisite lines I had, " by parcels," heard before, but " not intentively," and never did I hear them sung with such grace and spirit—never before did I behold the action so well suited to the word :—

> " Oh, its meeting is a pleasure,
>   Parting is a grief ;
> But an *on*constant *lovyer*
>   Is worse nor a thief !"

> " A thief and a robber
>   Your purse he will haave ;
> But an *on*constant *lovyer*,
>   He will bring you to the grave !"

I have no more room for criticism. These brief extracts will convince you that I have not decided in favour of the " River Melodies" on slight grounds. By some future opportunity

I will send you some more of them ; in the meanwhile I bid you good night, in the words
which the rowers are even now sounding in my
ears, as they tug at the oar, timing their strokes
to the cadence :

> "Some rows up, but we rows down,
> All the way to Shawnee town,
>   Pull away—pull away !"

LETTER V.

BLANNERHASSETT'S ISLAND, AND BURR'S CON-
SPIRACY.

WE left Parkersburgh early in the morning,
and in the course of the day passed Blannerhassett's Island, a spot which the intrigues of
one distinguished individual, the misfortunes of
another, and the eloquence of a third have
made classic ground. I would gladly have
loitered here for a few hours; but " time and
tide," says the old saw, " wait for no man."
How provoking! But time, and tide, and cap-
tains of keel-boats know nothing of the solici
tudes of sentimental travellers, and hurry us
away from a famous spot, with as little ceremony as from a half finished breakfast.

We approached the island in fine style, the
boatmen tugging manfully at the oar, and

straining their voices in concert. As we reached the upper end of it, they ceased their labours, and allowing the boat to float with the current, amused each other with stories of Burr and his confederates.

An event has seldom occurred, so intrinsically insignificant in its result, which has created so great a sensation as the conspiracy of Burr; which, indeed, derives its consequence principally from the celebrity of the names attached to it, and the ignorance of the world as to its final object. Burr was the rival of Hamilton; Hamilton the friend of Washington—his military aid, his political adviser, his social companion—equally eminent as a soldier, an orator, a writer, a financier, and a lawyer. The man who could make Hamilton experience, or even counterfeit,

> " The stern joy that warriors feel,
> In foemen worthy of their steel,"

must have stood far above mediocrity. Colonel Burr was the son of a gentleman, eminent for his learning and piety, for many years president of the most celebrated college in America; and was himself a man of transcendent genius, and

great attainments. He was remarkable for the
elegance of his manners, the seductiveness of
his address, the power and sweetness of his
eloquence ; but more so, perhaps, for the boldness and energy of his mind. Burr had contended unsuccessfully with Jefferson for the
presidential chair, which he lost by a single
vote ; but while he filled the second place in
point of dignity, few at that time would have
assigned him an inferior station in point of
talents.

The duel between Hamilton and Burr filled
the nation with astonishment and grief—grief
for the death of a great and useful man, and
astonishment at the delusion which occasioned
it. Burr, with the corpse of Hamilton at his
feet, might have felt the triumph of conquest ; but it was a momentary flush : the
laurels of the hero, watered by the tears of his
country, retained their verdure, and even those
who might have rejoiced at his political fall,
execrated the destroyer of his existence.

Shortly after this bloody catastrophe, the
conduct of Burr began again to excite the
attention of the public. He had resigned his

H

former employments, forsaken his usual haunts, and was leading an erratic and mysterious life. He frequently travelled *incognito*, performed long and rapid journeys, and remained but a short time at any one place. This restlessness was attributed to uneasiness of mind, and many began to sympathise with him whom they supposed to be thus tortured with the stings of conscience. But whatever might have been the workings of his mind, he soon evinced that his fire was not quenched, nor his ambition sated. He was now seen traversing the western wilds, eagerly seeking out the distinguished men of that country, particularly those who possessed military experience, or had hearts alive to the stirring impulses of ambition.

These indications were quickly succeeded by others of a more decided character. Secret as his intentions were, the first movement towards their execution awakened suspicion. The assembling of men, and collecting munitions of war roused the government to action. Burr was arrested,—his plans defeated, his adherents dispersed, and his reputation blasted. He became an exile, and a wanderer; and after

years of suffering, returned to his native land,
to become an insignificant member of that bar
of which he had been among the highest ornaments ; an obscure citizen of the country over
whose councils he had presided ; and to add
another to the list of splendid men who have
been great without benefit to themselves or
others, and whose names will be preserved only

" To point a moral, or adorn a tale."

He was entirely abandoned. Never was a
man more studiously avoided, more unani-
mously condemned. The voice of eulogy was
silent, the breath of party was hushed. Of the
many who had once admired and loved him,
none ventured to express their love or admiration. One fatal act of folly, or of crime, had
obscured all the brilliance of a splendid career ;
and although acquitted of treason by a court
of justice, a higher tribunal, that of public
opinion, refused to reverse the sentence which
consigned him to disgrace.

Such was the fate of Burr ; but his plans are
yet enveloped in mystery. A descent upon
some part of Spanish America, and the establish-

ment of an independent government, has been
stated to have been the object; but it is
alleged that a separation of the western states
from the Union formed a part of the project.
The latter charge rests almost entirely upon the
evidence of General Eaton, a gentleman whose
chivalrous disposition led him through many
singular adventures, and whose history, as recorded by himself, presents a more favourable
picture of his heart and genius than of his
judgment. He was a man of warm temperament, who adopted hasty and vivid impressions,
from the impulse of the moment. From his
testimony, I should be inclined to believe that
Colonel Burr had cherished some vague ideas
respecting a disjunction of the Union; but it
does not appear that those speculations were
ever matured into any settled plan, or confided
to his adherents. I am led to this conclusion
by the characters of Colonel Burr and the gentlemen who were implicated with him in his
disastrous expedition. Burr was a man of extended views, a close observer of men and manners, and it is not to be presumed that he would
have lightly embraced a scheme so fraught with

treason, madness, and folly. He knew the
American people well. He had studied them
with the eye of a statesman, and with the intense interest of an ambitious political aspirant.
His rank in society, his political station, and
his extensive practice at the bar, threw open a
wide and varied scene to his observation, and
exhibited his countrymen to him in a variety
of lights and shades.

Nor was Burr the man upon whom such opportunities would be lost. To him the avenues to
the human heart were all familiar, and he could
penetrate with ease into its secret recesses. To
study man was his delight—to study his countrymen his business. Could he then have been a
stranger to their intelligence, their sense of honour, their habits of calculation, and their love for
their republican institutions? Could he expect to
transform at once the habits, feelings, tastes, and
morals of a people conspicuous for their courage
and political integrity? - for such are the people
of the western states. It has been supposed,
and with some plausibility, that his hopes were
founded on the dissatisfaction evinced by the
western people at the time of the discussion of

our right to navigate the Mississippi. It is
true that the rude and unprovoked violation of
our privileges on that river by Spain excited
an universal burst of indignation throughout
the Union. It is also true, that this feeling
was most warmly displayed in the west. In
the Atlantic states, the insult was felt as impli-
cating our national honour; in the west it was
a matter of vital importance to all, and of personal interest to every individual, and as such
it came *home to men's business and bosoms.* The
Mississippi was the natural outlet, and New
Orleans the mart for the produce of the west;
and when that market, to which they believed
they had an indefeasible right of access, was
barred to them, it was but the natural and common impulse of the human mind which induced a people, at all times proud, impetuous
and tenacious, to call for vengeance and redress,
with a sternness and impatience commensurate
with their injuries. The conciliatory spirit and
tardy policy of Mr. Jefferson, neither satisfied
their feelings, nor suited their exigencies; and
they were willing to impute to tameness in the
executive, that which might have been the

result of parental solicitude. Believing themselves to be abandoned by the general government, they felt it a duty to protect their own
invaded rights; and if the government had not
interposed with effect, they would doubtless
have drawn the sword—against whom? the
government? No, but against the common
enemy. In this there was no treason nor disaffection—no estrangement from their sister
states, no breach of faith with the government,
nor violation of the compact. It was saying
only to their federal head—" Defend us, or
we will defend ourselves."

If Colonel Burr expected to fan these feelings
into rebellion, he had either more boldness or less
wisdom than has commonly been placed to his
credit; and had he openly avowed this project,
he would have called down upon his head the
imprecations of a people, who, if they had spared
his life, would not have forgiven so foul an insult
to their virtue and understanding. But let us
ask who were the adherents of Colonel Burr?
Who were they who were to share his fortunes,
to reap with him the proud laurels of successful valour, or the infamy of foul rebellion?

Were they persons of obscure name and desperate fortune, or were they men of good blood and fair fame—" the darlings of the nation ?" These questions are embarrassed with some uncertainty, because most of the gentlemen who have been accused of adhering to Colonel Burr, " giving him aid and comfort," have denied the fact; and as I am writing only for amusement, and speculating on events gone by, for speculation's sake, I wish not to assume any thing as a fact on this delicate subject, which is, or has been controverted. But it is not denied that many " prosperous gentlemen" were engaged in this enterprise; and many others suspected, with a belief so strong as to amount almost to certainty; and among these were men whom the people have since exalted to the most important trusts, and confided in with the most implicit reliance. Among them were men of high standing, who had reputations to be tarnished, fortunes to be lost, and families to be embarrassed; and many high-souled youths, whose proud aspirings after fame could never have been gratified amid the horrors of a civil war and the guilty scenes of rebellion.

It is argued against these gentlemen, that they have uniformly denied their connexion with Burr, which it is supposed they would not have done had they known his designs to be innocent. But this I do not conceive to be a fair argument. The united voice of the whole nation had declared Burr to be a traitor, and his adherents shared the obloquy which was heaped upon their misguided leader. Even admitting their innocence or their own belief of it, still it would have been a hopeless task for this handful of men to oppose their feeble asseverations to the "voice potential" of a whole people. Many of them, also, were candidates for office, and they found the avenues to preferment closed by the anathemas pronounced by the people against all who were concerned in what they believed to have been rank conspiracy. They might, therefore, have bent to the current which they could not stem. The apostle Peter denied his master thrice!—but was, nevertheless, a good honest apostle after all.

But I know that you are, by this time, ready to ask me, whether I am seriously endeavouring to convince you that Burr was a true and loyal subject to the sovereign people of these United States? I have no such design; though I must confess, that if I had the power to execute so difficult a project, I would with pleasure employ it. I should be happy to obliterate a stain from the annals of my country, and a blot from the fame of a fellow-citizen. I should be glad also to be always victorious in argument, if I could admit that success was the test of truth. But this I do not believe. I will tell you what I *do* believe. I believe that nine-tenths of Burr's adherents knew no more about his projects than you, and I, and all the world; and that those who do know any thing, to his or their own disadvantage, will be wise enough to keep their own counsel. But if I cannot tell you what Colonel Burr intended to do, I can relate what he did; for here I am in sight of the deserted fields and dilapidated mansion of the unfortunate Blannerhasset! That this fairy spot, created by nature in one of her kindest moods, and embellished by the hand of art, was once the elegant retreat of a philo-sophic mind, has already been told in language

which I need not attempt to emulate.   But
alas! I cannot now recognise the taste of Blannerhasset, or realise the paradise of Wirt.   All
is ruin, solitude, and silence!   They are gone
who made the wilderness to smile.

Blannerhasset was an Irish gentleman of
easy fortune—a man devoted to science, who
retired from the world, in the hope of finding
happiness in the union of literary and rural
occupation.   He selected this island as his
retreat, and spared no expense in beautifying
and improving it.   He is described as having
been retired in his habits, amiable in his propensities, greatly addicted to chemical studies,
and a passionate lover of music.   In this romantic spot, and in these innocent pursuits, he
lived ; and, to crown the enchantment of the
scene, a wife, who is said to have been lovely, even
beyond her sex, and graced with every accomplishment that could render it irresistible, had
blessed him with her love, and made him the
father of her children.   But Blannerhasset, in
an evil hour, became acquainted with Burr—he
imbibed the poison of his ambition, became
involved in his intrigues, and shared his ruin—

a ruin as complete, desolate and hopeless, as his former state had been serene and bright.

Whatever were Burr's intentions, it is certain that they embraced schemes so alluring or so magnificent as to win the credulous Blannerhasset from the abstraction of study and the blandishments of love. This island became the centre of operations. Here arms were deposited and men collected; and here, assembled round their watch fires, young gentlemen, who "had seen better days," and "sat at good men's feasts," endured all the rigours of the climate and the privations of a campaign, rewarding themselves in anticipation with the honours of war and the wealth of Mexico. Burr and Blannerhasset were the master spirits who planned their labours; Mrs. Blannerhasset was the light and life of all their social joys. If treason matured its dark designs in her mansion, here also the song, the dance, and the revel displayed their fascinations. The order of arrest was the signal of dispersion to this ill fated band; and it is said that the lovely mistress of this fairy scene, the Calypso of this enchanted isle, was seen at midnight "shivering on the

winter banks of the Ohio," mingling her tears
with its waters, eluding by stratagem the ministers of justice, and destitute of the comforts
of life, and the solace of that hospitality which
she had once dispensed with such graceful
liberality.

I believe it is not doubted that Burr intended
to have attempted the conquest of Mexico. A
large portion of the people of that country,
were supposed to be waiting only for a favourable opportunity to throw off the Spanish yoke.
The Americans, as their neighbours, and as
republicans, would it was thought be received
without suspicion; nor would Burr have unfolded his ultimate design until it should be
too late to prevent its accomplishment. He
would then have established a monarchy, at the
head of which would have been King Aaron
the First. I am told that the young gentlemen who were proceeding to join him, often
amused themselves on this subject; talking,
half in jest and half in earnest, of the offices
and honours which awaited them. Titles and
places were already lavishly distributed in anticipation; and Mrs. ——, who was an accom-

plished and sprightly woman, had arranged the dresses and ceremonies of the court. When the alarm was given, and orders were issued for the arrest of Burr and his adherents, they were obliged to resort to a variety of expedients to escape detection. At Fort Massac, and other places, all boats descending the river were compelled to stop and undergo strict examination, to the great vexation of boatmen and peaceable voyagers, who were often obliged to land at unseasonable hours. Very diligent inquiry was made for the lady I have just mentioned, who several times narrowly escaped detection, through her own ingenuity and that of her companions.

ADIEU.

LETTER VI.

TRAVELLERS, AND THEIR TREATMENT.

I HAD not been long on board the boat when I discovered that its progress was frequently so slow as to allow me to make short excursions on the shore. Such opportunities were too precious to be neglected. Accordingly, equipped in a light summer-dress, with a fowling-piece on my shoulder, I invaded sometimes one bank, and sometimes the other, waging war against the squirrels of Virginia, Ohio, or Kentucky, as was most convenient. Thus I gained sport and healthful exercise, and procured a grateful addition to my frugal meals. In these digressions, I frequently encountered the inhabitants, and could make inquiries respecting the country. At their cabins I could always procure a refreshing draught of milk, as well as a dish

of conversation: and if I had found nothing
else, I should have been compensated for my
trouble in gazing at the droves of chubby children, who are mentioned in the *Navigator* as
a staple commodity of the country. They are
almost as abundant as the squirrels; and as
plump and active as health, hard fare, and
exercise can make them. By walking at a
brisk pace along the shore, I could keep in
advance of the boat when the men were not
rowing, and could pop over the squirrels, talk
to the men, take a peep at the women, and
kiss the children, while jogging on my way.
This is pleasanter, and far more profitable, than
lolling in a stage-coach with one's arms folded,
or reading newspapers in the cabin of a steam-
boat; nor do I envy the traveller who would
not deviate from his path to chat with a backwoodsman, or peep at a Kentucky beauty.

On these occasions, I had opportunities of
examining into the correctness of some of the
assertions made by English travellers. They
describe our people in the humbler walks of
life as possessing a certain surly independence, which they delight to display on every

occasion, which induces them to insult a well dressed stranger, whenever they get an opportunity, and to render any services which they are called upon to perform, with an air of doing a favour ; so that while they pocket your money, they remind you that they are your equals. With regard to the want of affability alleged by foreigners, I can say, with sincerity, that I have travelled from the St. Lawrence to the Potomac, and from the shores of the Atlantic to those of the Mississippi, without observing it. I have never proposed a civil question to an American without receiving a civil answer ; and I have seldom entered his dwelling without partaking of its hospitality. I have more than once, in consequence of accidents to which all travellers are liable, been thrown upon the kindness of strangers ; yet never did I know my countrymen deny the sacred claims of a stranger in distress. At their taverns, or their private houses, a man of decent appearance and civil deportment will always be kindly and respectfully received. So long as he behaves like a gentleman, he will receive the treatment due to his character; his privacy

I

will not be interrupted, his feelings hurt, or
his peace disturbed. Whatever he asks for in
a civil manner, will be furnished him, if possible ; but if it cannot be procured, he must
take what he can get without complaining ;
for the moment he abuses the country, com-
plains of his fare, or attempts in any manner
to coerce 'or criminate those around him, he
excites a spirit which it is much more easy to
arouse than to allay.

It is to be recollected that in the United States
independence is not nominal—it is actual, defined,
and in the possession of every individual. It
is not confined to civil and political rights, but
extends to every sphere of human action ; we
are not only independent of foreign governments, as a nation, but of our rulers as a
people, and of each other as men. There is no
class so powerful, no individual so popular, as
to be able to carry a public measure over our
heads : the power is emphatically in *the people*,
who, while they cheerfully submit the ordinary
concerns of government into the hands of
leading men, who are better qualified to rule
than themselves, feel and know their own su-

premacy, and fail not to exercise it, whenever their interests are jeopardized. We have no individuals who are necessarily dependent upon others for support—no depressing poverty and overmastering wealth. The results are evident; those who are obliged to labour, or to serve others, can choose their occupations and their employers—can stipulate prices, and negociate for terms. Masters are more abundant than servants; there are more who wish to employ others, than to be employed; and as none are forced to earn a precarious livelihood, by pursuing a given calling, or serving a particular individual, the baseness of servility is unknown. Can a man be expected to cringe where he may bargain? or to fawn where he has only to name his hire, and perform his duty?

On the other hand, this entire equality of rights prevents that insolence on the part of inferiors which it has been supposed to generate. As there is no tyranny on the one part, there is no feeling of oppression on the other; and where there is no overbearing superiority, there can be no source of humiliation. Pride dare not insult poverty, because poverty is stronger than pride, and will trip up her heels if she

give herself airs. Where the rich never oppress
the poor—where the tenant of a tattered suit,
is not insulted by the jeers of his more fortunate
fellow worm, who is *clad in purple*, and fares
sumptuously—no jealousy is engendered, no
corroding hate is rankling at the heart of the
inferior, ready to burst forth upon the first
occasion ; there is nothing to resent, and therefore no resentment is displayed. In countries
where the poor are kept in subjection, where
they see distinctions, endure oppression, and
suffer insult, they may view the rich with
malignant hatred. Those who have been accustomed to such a state of society may believe
it to be universal ; and, speculating upon the
probable results of equal rights, and the effect
which the enjoyment of those rights would
have upon the manners and morals of the
ignorant, have imagined that to exist in fact,
which really exists only in their own theory. The
hypothesis is correct enough in the abstract ;
but when applied to us, it is removed from its
legitimate foundation, and built up upon
assumed positions and false estimates, and
becomes a " baseless fabric."

Englishmen, and indeed the gentlemen of

our cities, receive rough treatment in the west,
from their ignorance or intentional disregard of
these principles.   They go snarling through
the country, as if disdaining the soil on which
they tread, and literally *quarrelling with their
bread and butter*, although conscious that it is
the best which can be had.   Whether invited
to share the plain repast of the hunter, or
seated at the plentiful table of the hotel, they
are dissatisfied because they have not the deli-
cacies of an eastern city, and rail at the poverty
of the country and the coarseness of its provisions.   The individual who behaves in this
way is at once set down to be *no gentleman*,
for the people have acuteness to know that the
politeness of a well bred man will accommodate
itself to every society in which he may be
placed, will induce him to receive the coarsest
food with complacency, and to be grateful for
the most awkward attempts which evince a
desire to please ; but if these gentlemen are
not sufficiently well bred to know how to conduct themselves, prudence might dictate the
course for them to pursue.   A slight acquaintance with the temper of our people is sufficient
to convince the most careless observer, that

one of the leading traits in the character of a
western American, or, indeed an eastern one
is, " to give as good as he gets." With a
stranger, he is equally ready to shake hands or
to quarrel, as he finds him in the humour ; if
the traveller is good tempered, he treats him
well—if testy, he delights to tease him—if impudent, it is ten to one but he flogs him.
Sensible and civil men are well treated and
well pleased, while the captious man is vexed
and crossed at every step.

It is not to be forgotten, however, that you may
make remarks freely, in the west, if you do it
pleasantly. A gentleman who remarked in
one of their taverns that " he had been obliged
to eat *bacon* until he was ashamed to look a pig
in the face," was greeted with a smile ; but if
he had used any coarse language in regard to
that popular and respectable dish, the affront
might have been swallowed as reluctantly as
the bacon.

A writer in the Edinburgh Review says of
the people of the western country, " They are
hospitable to strangers, *because they are seldom
troubled with them,* and because they have
plenty of *maize and smoked hams.* Their hospi-

tality, too, is *always* accompanied with *impertinent questions*, and a *disgusting display* of *national vanity*." If the writer of this precious scrap had ever visited the country he libels, he would have known that it contains as many distinct falsehoods as could be conveniently crowded into so brief a paragraph. No country is more "troubled" with strangers than this; they swarm the land, spreading themselves over it in every direction; every stream is traced, every forest explored, and the taverns of every little village filled and overflowing with the crowds brought hither by emigration, by curiosity, or by business. Many of these are needy adventurers from the very land whose writers thus defame us, who, destitute of the means of subsistence, and ignorant of the country, are indebted to its inhabitants for food to support, and advice to guide their steps. The hospitality of the west, is best known to those who have experienced it :

> "Meat for keen famine, and the generous juice
> That warms chill life, her charities produce."

But if that hospitality is caused by the abun-

dance with which Heaven has blessed our prolific country, it springs from that which I suspect seldom troubles these Scotch gentry, and
whose charities, by the same rule, ought to be
very sparing.   The critic might have found
a better reason; it is that their hearts are as
generous as they are brave—the latter quality
not being denied them even in "the fast
anchor'd isle."   The same spirit which glowed
at Chippeway, on Lake Erie, and at New
Orleans, still illumines the shadows of our
western forests ; in war it produced daring
achievements—in peace it warms the heart to
deeds of charity and mercy.

If a foreigner, in passing through our country, grasps at every occasion to make invidious
comparisons, sneering at its population, manners,
and institutions, and extolling those of his own
native land, nothing is said of *national vanity.*
When it was determined in England to tear
the "striped bunting" from the mast-heads of
our "fir-built frigates" and to "sweep the
Yankee cock-boats from the ocean," no *national
vanity* was displayed at all ; when the very Review in question tells us that England is the

bulwark of religion, the arbiter of the fates of kingdoms, the last refuge of freedom, there is no *national vanity* in the business—not a spice. But if a plain backwoodsman ventures to praise his own country, because he finds all his wants supplied, and his rights defended, while he is not pestered with tax-gatherers and excisemen, is not devoured by fox-hunting priests, pensioners, and paupers, sees no dragoons galloping about his cottage, and is allowed to vote for whom he pleases to represent him—all of which he has good reason to believe is ordered differently in another country—this is a *" disgusting display* of *national vanity."* If he ventures to exhibit a shattered limb, or a breast covered with scars, and to tell that he received these honourable marks in defence of his native land, on an occasion when the *" best troops in the world"* fled before the valour of undisciplined freemen, led by a Jackson or a Brown, this is *very disgusting.*

The fact is, that English travellers, and English people in general, who come among us, forget that the rest of the world are not as credulous and *gullible* as themselves; and are

continually attempting to impose fictions upon
us, which we refuse to credit.   They seem not
to be aware, that we are a reading people, and
would convince us that they are a wise, valiant,
and virtuous people, beloved and respected by
all the world, while we are an ignorant idle set
of boobies, for whom nobody cares a farthing.
They tell us how happy and *comfortable* every
body is in England, and what a poor, forlorn,
forsaken, miserable set we are, who have had the
misfortune to be born in *a new country*, and
never saw a king, a lord, or a hangman.   One
of them told me that he had never heard of the
battle of New Orleans, until he came to
America several years after it was fought, and
that the British nation had hardly ever heard
of the war with America.   Now, when we refuse
to credit these things, and flatly deny them, as
we often do, we are set down as a conceited,
vain people, who presume to think for ourselves,
and to believe that we know something, when a
prating renegade or a venal reviewer shall
pronounce us fools.   John Bull forgets that his
own vanity is a source of merriment with the
rest of the world.

During my jaunt I have entered freely the meanest habitations, and conversed familiarly with the most indigent of the people; but never have I received a rude nor an indecorous reply. When I approached the door of the rudest hut, I was invited to enter, a seat was handed me, and if the family was eating, I was pressed to partake of their meal. However homely their fare might be, they neither seemed ashamed to offer nor unwilling to share it. At the little cabins along the river, we paid reasonable prices for bread, butter, milk, and other articles, which we purchased; but they seldom charged for what we ate in their houses; and when I penetrated a little farther into the country, among the respectable farmers, they seemed offended at being offered money for what we procured from them.

Returning from one of these excursions, I was overtaken by the night, and found my path obstructed by a deep inlet from the river, which being choked with logs and brush, could not be crossed by swimming. Observing a house on the opposite side, I called for assistance. A half naked, ill-looking fellow came down, and after dragging a canoe round from the river with some trouble, ferried me over, and I followed him to his habitation, near to which our boat was moored for the night. His cabin was of the meanest kind, consisting of a single apartment, constructed of logs, which contained a family of seven or eight souls, and every thing seemed to designate him as a new and unthrifty settler. After drinking a bowl of milk, which I really called for by way of excuse for paying him a little more for his trouble, I asked to know his charge for ferrying me over the water, to which he good humouredly replied, that he "never took money for helping a traveller on his way." "Then let me pay you for your milk." "I never sell milk." "But," said I, urging him, "I would rather pay you, I have money enough." "Well," said he, "I have milk enough, so we're even; I have as good a right to give you milk, as you have to give me money."

In my visits to these people, I sometimes inquired minutely respecting their employments, their prospects, and their health, and have always found them sufficiently communicative.

They not only spoke frankly of their own concerns, and of all that transpired within the little sphere of their own neighbourhood, but could, most of them, give accurate accounts of distant places. Their opinions are given promptly, and with the utmost sincerity, for nothing would be viewed among them with more indignation than an attempt to mislead a stranger. I was often, it is true, obliged to submit in return to a similar inquisition ; but it is the custom : and though the people are not intrusive or troublesome to those who do not seek their society, yet if you commence a conversation, they expect it to be continued upon terms of equality. A traveller might pass from Pittsburgh to St. Louis without being asked a question, except those relating to the state of roads or rivers, or such other subjects as strangers, when thrown together, may with propriety speak of to each other : true, he might meet with a wag, or an impudent fellow : but such an incident, which might happen in any part of the world, should not be allowed to have any bearing upon the character of a people.

The surly wight, therefore, who wrapt in
his reflections fancies himself journeying among
" strange cold hearts," and shrinks from an intercourse which he believes will produce him neither
benefit nor pleasure—whose suspicious temper
induces him to look upon human nature with
an eye of doubt and fear, or whose pride repels
the unauthorized familiarity of honest indigence
—who, in short, keeps a herald's office in his
own bosom, and measures his civilities according
to the rank of his companion—may enjoy the
solitude and taciturnity he covets. He might
even pass unnoticed, unless, indeed, a waggish
boatman should remark, as I heard one of them
on a similar occasion, that he " kept his mouth
shut for fear of getting his teeth sun-burnt."
How much more amiable is the conduct of the
tourist, who, feeling himself interested in the
country through which he is passing, and
knowing that he can only become acquainted
with its character by a familiar intercourse
with the people, endeavours to make himself an
acceptable guest in every circle ; who enters
into the diversions and employments of those
around him ; who looks on men as his fellow-

creatures, whose virtues please him, and whose vices he deplores; who accepts the hospitality of the peasant as cheerfully as that of the planter, and can say to each,

> " I take thy courtesy, by Heaven,
> As freely as 'tis nobly given !"

How amiable too, must be the character of that people, who, acting upon the rule that a polite deportment is the best letter of introduction, neither suspect nor repel the traveller who wears the exterior of decency and carries the stamp of candour in his visage; who make a companion of the stranger, and cheer the heart of the wayfaring man.

You must recollect, that the most secluded spots in this country are visited by intelligent strangers, who must naturally be desirous of examining into the very points which so many persons have traversed the land to investigate, and so many books have been written to explain. In the dwellings of the wealthy, such persons may remark the abundance, and admire the intelligence, which prevails; but they must seek in humbler scenes for *first causes* and *minute details;* they must trace out and analyse the distant fountain in its native cave, follow its sinuosities, and mark its accumulating course, before they are competent to delineate the distinct traits which form the character of the majestic stream. They inquire, therefore, into all the little details respecting the settler's origin, emigration, and settlement, the increase of his wealth and family, and the final result of his exertions. Now, certainly, it is not surprising that the man who is frequently required to answer such questions, should sometimes undertake to ask them; nor is it more so that a plain man should put his interrogatories in direct and rather homely language, such as, " Stranger, if it's no offence, what might be your father and mother's name? what parts are you from?" &c. This is natural enough in a free country; and as it evinces an honest independence, and shews that a man is not afraid of his guest, nor ashamed of himself, I confess I am not displeased with it. Every thing connected with the settlement, growth, and improvement of this country is interesting, as well to the traveller as to the inhabitant. Those

who have not the opportunity of gaining such
intelligence by their own observation, must
elicit it from others who have had that advantage ; and in such conversations they cannot
avoid being minute and *personal* in their inquiries. To form an opinion of the productive-
ness of the country, you must ask the settler
what property he brought with him, and how
much he has increased it; whether he works
himself, or hires labourers ; what wages he pays
his hirelings, and whether he gives them produce or money ; whether his wife makes her
own cloth or buys it, &c. To judge of the
climate by its effects on him and his family,
you wish to know to what latitude their constitutions had been previously accustomed ; and
you inquire the number and ages of his children, and their manner of living, in order to
decide whether their healthful or sickly appearance is attributable to the climate or to their
own habits. Now all these are impertinent
questions, which one gentleman has no right to
ask of another ; and he who puts them to our
sturdy citizens must expect the compliment to
be returned : but they are justified by the

K

motive, and that motive is well understood. The settler also wishes to know the destination of other emigrants, their opinion of the country they have left, and of that to which they are going; the progress of other settlements, compared with his own; the productions which succeed best, and the trades which flourish most. It is not, therefore, always an *idle* curiosity which leads him to inquire your rank, profession, and country; and when he asks your name, it is only an awkward way of introducing the subject. It should be added, that this inquisitive disposition, if it can be so called—this habit of asking *impertinent questions*, as the Edinburgh Reviewer will have it—is only found in new and thinly settled neighbourhoods, and amongst uneducated men. Throughout the older and better improved parts of the western country, the traveller would find himself sometimes in polished and always in civilized society, recognizing all the ordinary rules of decorum. But the *maize and smoked ham* he must be content to encounter, and he must be worse than a Jew who would quarrel with such fare. He will also find the rapid progress of the

American empire a constant theme of exultation—the policy, statistics, industry, and resources of the states, subjects of conversation. To those frequent and free discussions must we attribute that acuteness, and that knowledge of our country, for which the Americans, particularly those of the west, are remarkable. Foreigners may call this *national vanity :* so let it be : we *are* proud of our country, and are not ashamed to proclaim that pride : but so long as we do no worse than talk of ourselves and our own concerns, the tongue of the slanderer should be silent.

LETTER VII.

HARD NAMES; ANTIQUITIES; ANECDOTES.

FIVE miles below Blannerhassett's Island, is Little Hockhocking River; a little further on we have Hockhocking Island, and Great Hockhocking River. This would seem to be a family name among the streams and islets of this section, or at least to have been a favourite appellation among the first explorers of this region. It is rather a jaw-breaking word; but in common use it is softened by a device similar to that of the good lady in New England, whose son was named, " *Through-much-tribulation-we come-into-the-kingdom-of-heaven;* she called him ' *Tribby*,' for *shortness;*" and for the same reason, probably, the word " *Hocking*" has been substituted for its stately original. A town has been laid out at the mouth of the latter of these streams, called Troy; and on its banks, about twenty-five miles off, we find Athens, said to be a thriving village, with an academy, situated in a fine country. If Homer could be permitted to repass the Styx, would he not be amused at the sight of modern Troy and Athens on the shores of the Hockhocking? Think you a Grecian tongue could compass such a collection of harsh consonants?

Ten miles lower down, and near the mouth of *Shade River*, is the *Devil's Hole*, a remarkable cave on the Ohio side of the river. I had not time to visit this supposed residence of his satanic majesty, or to explore the banks of the modern Styx.

In the afternoon we passed Le Tart's Rapids. Here are some fine farms and handsome improvements. At the foot of the rapids is a floating grist-mill; the chief part of the machinery is erected on a large boat, resembling a common scow, which also supports one end of the shaft of the water-wheel; the other end is supported by a small sharp boat, lashed at a sufficient distance, and devoted to this purpose alone. On the other side of the scow, is a large boat, which receives the flour, corn, &c.; all of these are lashed firmly together, and fastened to the shore, and the water rushing between them propels the wheel. The bend of the river at this place is graceful, and adds to the interest of a very pleasing prospect.

We passed the *Rock of Antiquity* in the night, so that I could not inspect it. It stands at the water's edge on the right side of the river, about three miles below the Rapids, and takes its name from some ancient sculpture, which appears on its face, supposed to be the work of the aborigines. None of the figures are now intelligible but one, which represents a man in a sitting posture, smoking a pipe; our uncultivated predecessors have left so few memorials behind them, that the rudest and frailest of their monuments arrest attention. The rough penciling of a savage hand has excited as much interest as the precious relic of an Italian master. Even this sequestered rock has attracted the eye of the curious traveller. For my part, I am not fond of inanimate curiosities; but if I could restore the fire to the dark eyes, and the gloss to the raven locks of some of the

savage beauties, who once " wasted their
sweetness on the desert air" of these solitudes, I would gaze at their wild glances with
more delight than ever was felt by a virtuoso
in the pantheons or the catacombs. I love
monuments; but let them be breathing and
blushing monuments of animated clay; these are
noble objects—one of which is worth all the
mummies, *Egyptian heads*, and *Rob Roy purses*
in Christendom, and all the rocks and stones
that ever the ingenuity of one age piled up to
puzzle the curiosity of another.

During the same night, we passed the mouth
of the Kenhawa River, Point Pleasant, and
Galliopolis. On the Kenhawa, about seventy
miles from its mouth, salt water is found in
abundance, and of excellent quality; extensive
manufactories of salt have been in operation
here for many years. This river, however, will
be better known to the historian, from the
bloody engagement which took place near its
mouth in the year 1774, between the British,
under Lord Dunmore, and an Indian army of
the Shawanoe, Delaware, Mingo, and other
tribes. This war is more usually known under

the title of "Lewis's Expedition," from a
Virginia gentleman of that name, who was the
active and conspicuous leader, although Dunmore was the nominal commander. The Indian
force assembled here, was not less than a thousand warriors, a body more numerous than they
have usually been able to collect at any one
point against the whites. It was after this
battle, that Logan, a chief of the Delawares,
sent to Lord Dunmore the speech which has
rendered his name so celebrated, and which is
considered as one of the finest displays of eloquence upon record. Mr. Jefferson, who preserved this beautiful effusion of native feeling
in his *Notes on Virginia*, has been accused of
palming upon the world a production of his
own, by those who had no other ground for the
suspicion, than the force and feeling of the
composition itself, and who forgot that genuine
eloquence is not the offspring of refinement.
But all doubt on this subject has been long
since removed, by the testimony of officers who
were present when it was delivered, and who
many years afterwards remembered the impression made upon their minds by the affect-

ing appeal of the unlettered chieftain. There are, however, strong reasons for the belief, that Logan himself was deceived as to the part supposed to have been taken by Colonel Cressaf in the massacre of his family, and that some of Cressaf's men, in retaliation for an attack made previously by the savages upon some traders, perpetrated this murder without his knowledge. Cressaf, it is said, was not in the neighbourhood at the time, and could not have known of the sudden broil which produced a catastrophe so deeply to be deplored.

The town of Galliopolis, in Ohio, four miles below the mouth of the Kenhawa, is finely situated on a high bank, and commands a pretty view of the river. It was settled about thirty years ago by about a hundred French families, who sought an asylum from the political tempest which devastated their native country. They purchased a large tract of land from a company who had obtained a grant of it from the United States. But the company failing to fulfil the conditions of their contract, the land reverted to the government, and the unfortunate French found, too late, that they had been duped. Thus, landless and in a strange country, their situation was truly distressing; but Congress, with a munificence highly honourable to the nation, interposed to save them from ruin, and, by a grant of twenty-four thousand acres, indemnified them in part for their losses.

On the morning of the twenty-first we passed Guyundat Village, in the vicinity of which we found Big Guyundat River, Little Guyundat, and Indian Guyundat. This would seem to be as favourite a name as Hockhocking. Just below the village, we overtook one of those rude skiffs which frequently convey emigrants to the west. This was a small flat-bottomed boat, of the simplest construction, about twelve feet long, with high sides and a roof. As I was looking out for a friend, who in a moment of whim had embarked by himself, a few days before me, in a "frail tenement" like the one in sight, I took our small boat and rowed towards it, but was not a little surprised on approaching it, to discover, instead of a young gentleman, a grey-headed man, and as grey a headed woman, tugging deliberately

at the oars. This primitive couple looked as
if they might have been *pulling together* down
the stream of life for half a century, without
having grown tired of each other's company;
for while their oars preserved a regular
cadence, they were chatting sociably together,
and they smiled as they invited me into their
skiff. I confess I was astonished ; for, much
as I had seen of the carelessness with which
my countrymen undertake toilsome journies,
and the alacrity with which they change their
habitations, I was not prepared to behold
without surprise old age and enterprise travelling together: and when I learned that this
ancient couple were seeking a new home, I anticipated a tale of banishment and sorrow. The
days of their pilgrimage had not been *few and
evil.* Neither of them could have seen much
fewer than sixty years, and both were withered,
wrinkled, and apparently decrepit ; but they
were sprightly and social, and spoke of clearing
new lands in the wilderness, with a confidence
which evinced nothing of the feebleness or in-
decision of old age. In answer to my inquiries,
as to the reasons which had suggested a change

of residence, the old man observed, in a careless, off-hand sort of way, " Why, Sir, our boys are all married, and gone off, and bustling about for themselves ; and our neighbours, a good many of 'em's gone *out back*, and so the old woman and me felt *sort o' lonesome*, and thought *we'd* go too, and try *our* luck."

"But, my friend, it's rather late in the day for you to become a wanderer."

" Tut, man," said he," better late than never —*there's luck in leisure*, as the saying is—and may be the old woman and me'll have as good luck as any of them."

This was followed by a tender of the whisky bottle ; and after drinking to our better acquaintance, should we meet again in the woods, we parted. Tell me no more of *antiquities ;* repeat not that this is a degenerate age! Here were the right sort of *antiquities.* This old Kentuckian, who at the age of sixty, still dares the gloom of the forest, panting for newer lands to settle, is worth a hundred dead Greeks or living Scotch Reviewers.

22d. This morning we passed Portsmouth, a small village in the Sciota bottom. A little below this I landed at a cabin, where the good woman was nursing a child with a sore head. She firmly believed that the eruption could not be cured, except by a seventh son.

On the 23d we passed Maysville, in Kentucky, where I landed to throw some letters into the post-office, but had not time to make any observations.

About sunset we landed our boat on the Kentucky shore. A poor negro, who had lost both his feet, but still moved with activity on his knees, like the warrior in Chevy Chace, who,

> " When his legs were smitten off,
> Still fought upon his stumps,"

came on board to dispose of a string of fish. One of the passengers, an European, whom we had picked up lately, purchased a fishing line from him, directing the fellow to call again for the money ; but when he came, refused to pay the stipulated sum, and kept the poor black wrangling half an hour about a few cents. The needy cripple was at last compelled to take what he could get, and hobbled away,

muttering imprecations against the stranger,
whom he termed "a mighty poor white man;"
an expression which, in the mouth of a negro,
indicates the most sovereign contempt. The
blacks entertain a high respect for those whom
they term "gentlemen," and apply that title
with a good deal of discrimination; but "poor
white folks" they cordially despise. I regretted
the conduct of our fellow-passenger, because
such meanness and dishonesty disgust the
person who suffers by it, and induces him, on
subsequent occasions, to treat foreigners with
less civility: and it is thus that the miscon-
duct of travellers provokes our people into acts
of rudeness, which make them appear disad-
vantageously to those who are unacquainted
with the cause of it. It was a vile act. The
man who would cheat a negro would purloin
without shame; he who would wrong a poor
cripple, would not hesitate to commit murder.
Had he been an American, I should have
blushed for him; as it was, I could only thank
Heaven he was not my countryman.

LETTER VIII.

BIOGRAPHY OF GENERAL PRESBY NEVILLE.

You will have seen already that it is not my intention to confine this correspondence within the limits of any fixed plan, or to enter into any of those elaborate details which belong to more patient, or more learned investigators. I shall not lay down courses and distances, analyze minerals, or describe the volant or the creeping tribes ; but when an amusing anecdote or a precious morsel of biography presents itself, I shall preserve it with the zeal of a *virtuoso*. You may smile when I mention biography as among the subjects of interest in a *western tour ;* but you have yet to learn that your tramontane countrymen cherish among them many names which deserve a place upon the brightest page of American history ; and that

those rocky barriers, which until recently have
repelled the tide of emigration, have concealed
behind them patriots and heroes, whose deeds
would give dignity to any age or country.
Among these, not the least conspicuous was a
gentleman whose name is familiar to me from
its connexion with the traditions current
among the inhabitants of that part of western
Pennsylvania in which I have resided for several years past.   His history recurred to me this
morning as we passed the village of Neville.

Here were passed in seclusion the last years
of a man who had shone in the brightest circles,
and borne a conspicuous character in public
life.   General Presby Neville was born in
Virginia in the year 1756; he received the rudiments of his education at Newark academy, in
Delaware, and graduated at the University of
Pennsylvania in 1775, when he received an
honour, and spoke the Latin *Salutatory* in the
presence of the American Congress.   Immediately after leaving college, he abandoned the
idea of one of the learned professions, with a
view to which he had been educated, and joined
a company commanded by his father, the late

General John Neville, then stationed at Fort Pitt. The latter gentleman was promoted about this time to the rank of Lieutenant Colonel, in Colonel Wood's regiment of the Virginia line, and his son obtained command of the Colonel's company, with rank of Captain Lieutenant. He marched to Boston in 1775; and passed through all the grades to the rank of Lieutenant Colonel. He was at the battles of Brandywine, Germantown, Monmouth, Princeton, and Trenton, and indeed in most of the distinguished actions which occurred, and was finally taken prisoner at the surrender of Charleston in South Carolina, and remained on parole until the end of the war.

In the early part of his service, he was aid-de-camp to Major General Stevens, whom he shortly after left, " to follow to the field a warlike lord." La Fayette was then a popular chief; his youth, his rank, his gallantry, his foreign lineage, and his zeal in the republican cause, threw an air of romance about his achievements which rendered him the favourite hero of every circle, while his amiable deportment and polite accomplishments endeared him

to his friends. He was the mirror by which old
men advised the youthful champions of that
day to shape their manners.   Invited into his
family in the capacity of aid-de-camp, Colonel
Neville became the bosom friend and companion in arms of the gallant Frenchman.   He
remained with him three years, sharing with him
the toils of war, the triumphs of victory, and the
gratitude of emancipated thousands.   Community of danger and similarity of taste produced
an   ardent   friendship   between   these   young
soldiers, which was not damped by separation,
nor   cooled   by the shadows of old age.   La
Fayette, after spending the morning of his life
in deeds of virtuous daring, retired to his native
country, to devote its evening to philosophic
repose.   Neville remained on the busy scene,
but an intimate correspondence was kept up
between them until the death of the latter.

At the close of the revolutionary war,
General Neville married the daughter of the
celebrated General Daniel Morgan, and removed to Pittsburgh, where he spent many
years in affluence and happiness, such as
rewarded the labours of but few of the veteran

founders of our republic. Here he was elected
to the General Assembly, once it is believed by
an unanimous voice, and always by such over-
whelming majorities, as sufficiently showed his
unbounded and merited popularity. He continued to represent the county of Alleghany,
until his fondness for domestic life induced
him to retire. He was several times nomi-
nated as a candidate for Congress, but always
declined the service.

But I am inexcusable in detaining you so long
with a detail of these honours, which are, or
ought to be, only the ordinary rewards of merit:
so true it is that in contemplating the trappings
of wealth and office, we forget the merits of
the wearer. The most captivating traits in the
character of General Neville are yet untold—
to depict them, we must pass his threshold, and
observe him in that circle of which he was the
centre, soul, and life. We have seen that he
was not only himself a revolutionary hero, but
was the son of a gallant soldier, and the son-in-
law of one of our most distinguished leaders.
Imbibing thus a military spirit with his dearest
associations, his whole heart was filled with

chivalric ardour. Fresh from the study of
Greek and Roman models, he had plunged into
the horrors of a civil war, with a mind teeming
and glowing with classic images of military
and civic virtue, and he had the rare felicity of
realizing the visions of his fancy; in Washington, Hamilton, and La Fayette, he saw Athenian
elegance, combined with Spartan virtue; while
Rome, in the maturity of her fame, was eclipsed
by the youthful vigour of American valour.
These events, operating on a young and ardent
heart, contributed to nourish and expand a
romantic loftiness of feeling, which gave a tone
to the character and fortunes of the future
man. He thought, felt, and acted with the
pride, the enthusiasm, and the energy of a
soldier, but he also acted, felt, and thought on
every occasion with that benevolence which is
so attractive in the character of a truly brave
man, and with that courtesy which belongs
exclusively to the well-bred gentleman. No
man could boast more from family and fortune,
yet no man ever wore his honours with more
becoming gracefulness. He was a proud man,
but his pride was as far above the vanity of

unmeaning distinctions, as his heart was above
fear, and his integrity above reproach.   He was
the kindest of human beings ; there were a
thousand tendrils about his heart, that continually entwined themselves in the little world
around him.   His fancy often roved abroad
with the classic poet, and loved to linger with
the heroes of other days; but his affections
were always at home.   No man was too great
for his friendship, none too insignificant for his
kindness.   His understanding was strong, and
highly cultivated ; he was a lover and patron
of the arts ; elegant in his manners, and easy
in his conversation.

The house of General Neville was the seat
of festivity, and hospitality smiled at its portals.
It was resorted to by the gentry of those days,
as a temple consecrated to conviviality and
intellectual enjoyment, whose shrine was always
accessible.   The Cerberus which modern
fashion has placed at the doors of the wealthy,
to snarl at indigent merit, was then unknown ;
nor had the heartlessness of the *bon ton*, contrived that ingenious system of *pasteboard civilities*, by means of which the courtesies of social

intercourse are now so cheaply paid and received. The hospitalities of that day were
substantial, and never were they dispensed with
more profusion than under the roof of General
Neville. Pittsburgh and its vicinity were then
but thinly populated, and houses of entertainment were scarce. Strangers of respectability
almost always brought letters of introduction
to the General, to whose house they were
invited with a frankness which banished all
reserve on the part of the guest. Here they
remained during their stay in the country; and
such was the hearty welcome they received,
and the continued round of social pleasure
which they enjoyed, that their visits were often
delayed beyond the original limit. But it was
not under his own roof alone that this gentleman dispensed happiness; he was the constant
patron of merit, and the needy never appealed
to him in vain for relief.

A man so highly gifted was not calculated
to pass unnoticed through life; nor was all
his time devoted to its enjoyment. Besides
the offices which he exercised, he was in other
respects an active citizen; a liberal promoter

of all public improvements, and a careful guardian of the rights of his fellow-citizens. He was often referred to by the Federal Government for local information; and was once appointed on a mission to France, but was taken ill at Boston, where he was about to embark, and obliged to decline the duty. He also, at different periods, held the offices of surveyor, county lieutenant, and paymaster general to the army of the insurrection. These trusts he discharged with fidelity. The friendship of Washington and of most of the conspicuous men of that day, which he had gained as a soldier, he forfeited not as a citizen.

Such was the man who was doomed in his old age to present a striking example of the instability of fortune. His notions were too princely for a private individual, and adversity was the inevitable consequence. His fine fortune dwindled under his lavish beneficence, and was perhaps more deeply injured by those who shared his bounty, and whom he trusted without suspicion. There was no guile in him, and he suspected it not in others. He found himself, at last, dependent in a great measure for support upon an office which he held under the state of Pennsylvania. But even this was not left to him. It would have been inconsistent with the practice of those times to have allowed an old soldier to carry his grey hairs in peace to the grave. Party spirit had reared its gorgon head, and as merit is ever the first object of its vengeance, the revolutionary veteran had nothing to hope. But his sun was already setting, and the twilight of his existence alone was darkened by the storm. Still it was a sad reverse.

> "The harp that once in Tara's halls,
>   The soul of music shed,
>   Now hung as mute on Tara's walls,
>   As if that soul was fled."

Thus deprived of all but an unsullied reputation, General Neville retired to this spot, and seated himself on the land which had been earned by his revolutionary services. Here he lived in indigence, and died in obscurity. His remains were removed to Pittsburgh by the filial care of his eldest son, where they were interred with the highest military and civic honours.

I was at the burial of that gallant man. While living I never saw him, but I wept at his grave. It was a touching scene. That man in prosperity was idolized; in adversity, forsaken; in death, honoured. There were those around his last earthly receptacle whose feet had long forgotten the way to his dwelling; but there were none who remembered not his virtues. There were those who had drank of his cup, and whose hearts had smote them at that moment, could they have felt, as that sleeping warrior had felt, "how sharper than the serpent's tooth is man's ingratitude." The young soldiers, whose nodding plumes bent over the corpse, had been the infants who had played about the good man's path, and now remembered only his grey hairs and his gallant name; there was a flush on their cheeks, but it arose from the reflection, "that the dearest tear that Heaven sheds, is that which bedews the unburied head of a soldier."

LETTER IX.

SCENERY—CINCINNATTI—GENERAL ST. CLAIR—
PROGRESS OF IMPROVEMENT.

As we continue to descend the river, its
shores still exhibit the same interesting character which I have heretofore described.   The
hills still present their bold outlines, and the
vales their shadowy recesses.   But as the season
advances, the forest is seen rapidly discarding
the dark and dusky habiliments of winter, and,
assuming its vernal robes, it blooms forth with
renovated life and lustre.   The gum tree is
clad in the richest green ; the dogwood and
redbud are laden with flowers of the purest
white and deepest scarlet ; the locust bends
with the exuberance of its odorous blossoms.
On the southern sides of the hills the little
flowers are peeping forth, while winter barely

retains a semblance of her recent dominion over the northern exposures. The oak, the elm, the walnut, the sycamore, the beech, the aspen, the hickory, and the maple, which here tower to an incredible height, have yielded to the sunbeams, and display their bursting buds and expanding leaves. The tulip-tree waves her long branches, and her yellow flowers high in the air. The wild rose, the sweet-briar, and the vine, are shooting into verdure; and, clinging to their sturdy neighbours, modestly prefer their claims to admiration, while they give early promise of fruit and fragrance. The fountains, gushing from the hill side in profuse libations, come rippling over the rocks in limpid currents, forming cascades and pools, while the smoke rising from the distant cabin, reminds the traveller of

" ———— the blest abode,
Of Edward and of Mary."

Blame me not for yielding, amid such scenes, to the influence of feeling, and giving up my whole soul to wild, and warm, and visionary

fancies. It is a humiliating reflection that our
sweetest hours are those which are least useful
and least connected with the realities of life;
but it cannot be denied, that the only unmingled
happiness that we enjoy is in those hours of
mental abstraction, when the heart, revelling in
its own creations, forgets the world with its
vanities and cares. For my part I would rather
glide silently along the smooth current of the
Ohio, lie extended upon the deck at eve,
gazing at the last rays of the sun, dimly discovered on the tops of the tallest trees, or
behold the morning beams of the great luminary
sparkling among the dew-drops, than sit upon
a throne and be debarred of such exquisite
enjoyments!

We arrived at Cincinnatti in the morning;
but when I inform you that we remained here
only a few hours, and that the greater part of
this time was spent with a friend, and that
friend a lovely female, a companion of my
dancing days, you will not be surprised if I
add, that I have nothing to relate concerning
this town. Those days may be over with me
in which the violin could have lured me from

the labour of study, and the song from the path
of duty; but never, if I know myself, will that
hour come when woman shall cease to be the
tutelary deity of my affections, the household
goddess of my bosom! Think me an enthusiast,
or a great dunce, if you please—but never, I
pray, if you love me, believe that I could think
of statistics with a fair lady at my side, or that
I could hoard up materials for a *Letter from the
West*, while a chance presented itself to talk
over my old courtships, and dance once more
my old cotillons. No, no; this correspondence
may be fun to you, and nuts to our friend Mr.
Oldschool, who are but readers of these poor
sheets of mine, and endure not the pains of the
authorship thereof; but setting that aside, I
would not give one " merry glance of mountain
maid," for the plaudits of the literary world.
You will remind me, I dare say, of posterity :—
but, in the language of a merry neighbour of
mine, I reply, " Hang posterity! what did
posterity ever do for me!" So I shall write
when I please, and court the girls when I can.

I had only time therefore to discover, that I
was in a town of ample size, and goodly appear-

ance, where I met genteel forms and busy
faces. The harbour was crowded with boats,
the wharfs covered with merchandise, the
streets thronged with people. The indications
of wealth, of business, and refinement, were too
striking to pass unobserved, by one who re-
flected how recently the forest frowned upon
this spot.

We left Cincinnatti in the afternoon. As
the town faded from my sight, and the shadows
of the forest gathered again around me, I was
struck with the sudden contrast. Instead of
paved streets and splendid buildings, the re-
treats of science and the marts of business, the
hum of men and the rattling of carriages, I
saw only the glassy tide and its verdant shores,
and heard no sounds save those of the wood-
pecker, the squirrel, and the mocking-bird.
The hand of man had not yet shorn the hill of
its green covering; its " budding honours"
were " thick upon it." Here was a fine specimen of the pristine luxuriance of nature ; behind me a noble monument of art. But these
are miniature scenes, which are chiefly interesting, as they lead the mind to a larger field of

speculation, and as they exhibit " counterfeit presentments" of the rapid changes which have been operating far and wide throughout this extensive region.

Thirty years ago, the American forces, commanded by General St. Clair, were defeated by the savages in the territory north-west of the Ohio. The brilliant talents of this brave soldier, were exerted in vain in the wilderness. The wariness and perseverance of Indian warfare, created every day new obstacles and unforeseen dangers ; the skill of the veteran was baffled, and undisciplined force prevailed against military science. The art of the tactician proved insufficient when opposed to a countless multitude, concealed in the labyrinths of the forest, and aided by the terrors of the climate. The defeat of our army became the subject of investigation by a military tribunal; and if any proof had been wanting of the ability of its commander, his defence before the court martial must have afforded that testimony. But this gentleman, like the unfortunate Burgoyne, exerted his eloquence in vain ; he was admired, blamed, applauded, and condemned ! The dis-

tinguished reputation gained by General St.
Clair in the revolutionary war was insufficient
to sustain him under this reverse of fortune.
His popularity declined, his abilities were
doubted, and his services no longer required.
He retired to an obscure residence among the
mountains of Pennsylvania. Here, in the most
abject poverty, in a miserable cabin, upon a
sterile and dreary waste, among rocks and precipices, (fit emblems of his career!) he dragged
out a wretched existence, visited only by his
sorrows,—except when a solitary traveller, im-
pelled by curiosity to witness that which one of
the ancients has pronounced to be a noble
spectacle, penetrated the intricacies of the
Laurel Mountain to behold a great man in
adversity. Here he might be found, beyond
the reach of persecution, but not enjoying the
dignity of retirement, nor the sweets of domestic
life : for even here adversity had pursued this
unhappy man, and added the most distressing
private calamities to the already teeming burthen
of his sorrows. The general who had commanded armies, the governor who had ruled a
province, the patriot who had nobly dared in

the noblest of causes, endured these calamities in the country which had witnessed his deeds, and reaped the harvest of his exertions. He endured them without a friend to soften his bitterness, without a domestic to administer to his wants. Such is the fate of an *unsuccessful leader*, over whose fate the passage of a single cloud obscures the brilliance of a long career of glory, and is followed by ruin, darkness, and desolation! Sometimes he emerged from his solitude to make fruitless appeals to the justice of his country. His claims for the reimbursement of pecuniary advances made for the public cause, and for remuneration for services performed, were long disregarded. A short time before his death, the aged man, bending under the weight of fourscore years, appeared again at the metropolis, charming the young with his gaiety, the old with his wisdom—exhibiting a versatility of genius which few possess, and displaying a vigour of intellect, little consonant with his age, his sorrows, and his infirmities.

The late war had revived the enthusiasm of the nation. The ardour which once glowed in the bosom of our fathers, now swelled the veins of their children ; and while Congress was dis. tributing honours with a prodigal hand among the youthful heroes of 1814, the veteran of seventy-six appeared. The appeal was irresistible ; his claim was allowed—allowed, alas! when the worn-out soldier had reached the last out-post of his earthly pilgrimage !

General Wayne succeeded to the command, but not to the fate of St. Clair. By dint of rigid discipline, indefatigable exertion, and above all, a talent for Indian warfare, he redeemed the frontier settlements from destruction, and inflicted a heavy vengeance upon our tawny neighbours. The memory of Wayne (with that of General Butler, who fell in these wilds) is deservedly cherished by the western people. So marked has been their gratitude, that there is not a state or territory, west of the mountains, which has not named towns and counties after these gallant men. The name of St. Clair also occurs frequently on the map.

I have made this digression, to shew how recently our brave soldiers have sought " the bubble reputation at the cannon's mouth," on

the fields where the plough, the loom, and
shuttle, are now in peaceful operation, as well as
the importance of the contest in which they were
engaged. That enemy must have been far from
insignificant, in encountering whom St. Clair
or Wayne could reap obloquy or honour. The
states of Ohio, Indiana, and Illinois, have since
been formed out of portions of the country so
recently the theatre of war, and the territory
of Michigan organised for the purpose of temporary government.

So lately as the year 1794, troops were stationed throughout this country, for the protection of travellers passing down the river to
the distant settlements of New Orleans and
Kaskaskia, and for the security of the frontiers ; boats descending the river were manned
and armed, as for a dangerous enterprise, and
an attempt to traverse the wilderness was
considered as an effort of more than ordinary courage. On the same river, steam-boats,
for the transportation of passengers and merchandise, were in successful operation before
their introduction into Europe ; and the traveller may now enjoy the very luxuries of tra-

velling, where a few years ago the hardiest manhood sunk under its toils and perils.

In 1794, beasts of prey prowled over this region unmolested, and the savage was "monarch of all he surveyed," and "lord of the fowl and the brute." In 1810, the state of Ohio contained a population of two hundred and thirty thousand seven hundred and sixty souls, and the value of her domestic manufactures, according to the census, was one million nine hundred and eighty seven thousand, three hundred and seventy dollars. In 1815, the lots, lands, and dwelling-houses in Ohio, were valued at upwards of sixty-one millions of dollars; and in 1820, the marshal reported her population to be five hundred and eighty-one thousand four hundred and thirty-four souls.

Kentucky was first explored in 1770; the first settlement was made in 1775. In 1810, that state contained a population of four hundred and six thousand five hundred and eleven souls, and her manufactures were valued at four millions, one hundred and twenty thousand six hundred and eighty-three; and in 1820, the marshal's return of her population was five hundred and sixty-four thousand three hundred and seventeen souls.

In short—to close a parallel which may become tedious—from this land, so lately a wilderness, the savage has been expelled; towns and colleges have arisen; farms have been made; the mechanic arts cherished; the necessaries of life abound, and many of its luxuries are enjoyed. All this has been effected within the memory of living witnesses. Such are the fruits of civilization, and so powerful the effect of American enterprise!

LETTER X.

FRONTIER MANNERS.

I HAVE remarked at the little towns at which I have touched in this country, that the appearance of a stranger does not excite the same degree of curiosity which we observe in the villages of the eastern and middle states, and particularly at those which are not on the great mail routes. In those places, the arrival of a well-dressed stranger is a matter of general interest, and peculiarly so, if his apparel, or travelling equipage, be a little finer than usual, or if he assume any airs of importance ; the smith rests upon his anvil, the gossip raises her spectacles, and the pretty maidens thrust their rosy faces through the windows to gaze at the new comer. This propensity has been impressed on my memory, by the inconvenience it has sometimes produced, and the pleasure it has frequently afforded me.

The pretty hamlets of New England as well as those which are more thinly scattered through the western part of the state of New York, or along the banks of the Delaware and the Susquehanna, in Pennsylvania, are distinguished for their rural beauty, neatness, and simplicity. On entering one of these at the close of a summer-day, when the villagers sat about their doors and windows, to enjoy the coolness of the evening breeze, I have checked my horse, and hanging carelessly on my saddle, have passed slowly along, gazing with delight at the blooming cheeks and sparkling eyes, that have been directed towards me from every quarter. I have always had a wonderful predilection for handsome faces, and I do verily believe that if my breast were darkened by the heaviest sorrows, the rays of beauty would still strike to its inmost recesses, and there would still be a something there to refract the beams. But it cannot be expected that so erratic a being as myself, should ever be very sad or serious; the traveller must leave his heavy thoughts behind

him, with his heavy baggage, and keep a vacant
place for a thousand pleasing, novel, nick-nack
ideas, which he may pick up by the way.

Imagine such a wanderer, after jogging the
livelong day, in the scorching sun, over crags
and cliffs, or through mud and dust, with no
companion but the beast he bestrides—who,
however affable his disposition may be, is less
companionable than one could wish—arriving,
with " spattered boots" and a weary frame, at a
romantic village that has not a soul in it whom
he either knows or cares for. His fancy is
his world, for he has nothing to do with the
realities around him; he is not interested in
the vices, he knows not the distresses, he tastes
not the pleasures of those about him; he gazes
on them as the philosopher views a beautiful
insect, or inspects a lovely flower; he has no
feeling in common with the objects of his observation, but they afford him matter of pleasing reflection. The sun has just gone down,
the flowers have reared their drooping heads,
and the girls let fall their twining ringlets;
they have put on their best bibs and tuckers,
and their most amiable looks; the tea-table is

set, and the village beaux are congregated ; the old gentlemen, gathered in groups, are grumbling at the present state of affairs, while the young ones seem to be enjoying it, or making arrangements to change it for the better. Then to see those dimpled cheeks, laughing eyes, and ruby lips all displayed at once to the astonished glance of the " way-worn traveller," whose eye rests on nothing but white frocks and rosy faces ! I have found my heart more gladdened by such a scene, and my eye more pleased, than when from the summits of our Pennsylvanian mountains I have gazed upon the romantic vales below, or from the high-lands looked down upon the Hudson.

There are those who, to enjoy much less innocent and less ecstatic pleasures, would give all they possessed, curse their country, and turn Turks ; but they are miserable connoisseurs who purchase enjoyment at expensive prices, when nature spreads her table gratis. Thus I have extracted pleasure from a source which has afforded vexation to others ; a transient glance at the smiling faces of those pretty girls, has fully compensated me for the fatigue of answering, on arriving at an inn (if in New England) the tedious inquiries, whether I was a *southerner*, or a *York-state man*, and whether I was going *down south*, or *a way out back*.

If this be the case in our snug little rural towns, whose inhabitants enjoy the luxuries of society, and where the more wealthy part of them aspire to something like *style* among themselves, how much more would it be expected in these distant and lonely regions, where a town is usually composed of a few rude cabins, hastily erected on the margin of a river, and surrounded by extensive forests. Would you not suppose that a well dressed gentleman would be considered here as a natural curiosity, whose appearance would create a sensation as lively as that produced by the arrival of the elephant or the royal African tiger; and that a fashionable fair would rival the popularity of the Albiness, or the waxen figure of the Boston beauty? As for a dandy, can you believe he would be suffered to run at large, and not encaged and exhibited as a monster? But such curiosity is here somewhat rare, and the absence of it is easily accounted for: the fact is, that, insulated and lonesome as these spots appear, they are visited frequently by a great number and a great variety of people. The merchants, who make their annual journies to an eastern city to purchase goods ; the innumerable cara-vans of adventurers, who are daily crowding to the west in search of homes, and the numbers who traverse these interesting regions from motives of curiosity, produce a constant suc-cession of visitors of every class, and of almost every nation. English, Irish, French and Ger-mans, are constantly emigrating to the new states and territories ; and all the eastern, south-ern, and middle states send them crowds of inhabitants ; nor is it the needy and unfortunate alone who bury themselves among the shadows of the western forests.

There was a time, indeed, when the word *emigration* carried with it many unpleasant sensations ; and when we heard of a res-pectable man hieing to an unknown land, to seek a precarious existence among bears and musquitoes, we fancied that we saw the hand of a land speculator beckoning him to destruction, and pitied his fate. We are apt to imagine that these land-jobbing gentry were surrounded by retainers pretty much like those of David when he sojourned in the cave of Adullam, " and every one that was *in distress*, and every one that was *in debt*, and every one that was *discontented*, gathered themselves unto him, and he became a captain over them." But this is not the fact now ; whatever might have been the case a few years ago, we now find classes of people among the emigrants who would not be easily deluded. Gentlemen of wealth and intelligence, professional men of talents and education, and respectable farmers and artizans, have, after dispassionate inquiry, determined to make this country their future abode. Like Lot, " they lifted up their eyes, and beheld all the plain of Jordan, that it was well watered every where ;" fertile, " even as the Garden of Eden," and abounding in the choicest gifts of nature.

Thousands, it is true, have been driven here by want, from countries less congenial to the needy ; but though in some cases, their poverty and not their wills consented to the change, they have generally found it an advantageous one. Thus it is, that although in travelling you often meet the native woodsman with his hunting-shirt and rifle, you as often encounter persons of a different character ; and on arriving at a cabin, it would be difficult to guess what may be the particular description of its inhabitant. It is natural, therefore, that the sight of a stranger should have ceased to be wonderful where it is no longer rare ; and that no singularity of dress or appearance should excite the curiosity of those who are in the daily habit of seeing every variety of people.

For nearly the same reasons you will find few people in the west who are ignorant of the geography of their own country ; they all know something of the general description of even the most distant parts of the union. Many of them have emigrated from afar ; some travel over an immense extent of country from mere curiosity, or in search of the most eligible place *to settle* ; and others take long journies on mercantile and other speculations. They are acute observers ; and the most illiterate are seldom dull or ignorant. In the neighbourhood of Pittsburgh you will meet but few persons who cannot give you some idea of the route to Detroit or to New Orleans, and a tolerably correct notion of the intermediate country. Such knowledge is more or less general throughout the western country. All have travelled; and the information thus collected is communicated from one to another in their frequent discussions on the subject which is most common, and most interesting to them—the comparative advantages of the different sections of the country. In short, you will scarcely meet an old woman who cannot tell you that Pittsburgh is full of coal and smoke; that in New Orleans the people play cards on Sunday; that living is dear at Washington City, and cod-fish cheap at Boston; and that Irishmen are " plenty" in Pennsylvania, and pretty girls in Rhode Island.

LETTER XI.

SCENERY, SCIENCES, AND FIDDLING.

THE character of the scenery,—or as Lady Morgan would say, the physiognomy of nature, still exhibits the same appearance, as we continue to descend the river, which I have heretofore attempted to pourtray, except that the hills are gradually becoming less bold and rocky. The shores of the Ohio do not any where present that savage grandeur, which often characterises our larger streams. No tall cliffs, no bare peaks or sterile mountains, impress a sentiment of dreariness on the mind. The hills are high, but gracefully curved, and every where clothed with verdure. There is a loneliness arising from the absence of population, a wildness in the variegated hues of the forest, and in the notes of the feathered tribes ;

but the traveller feels none of that depression
which results from a consciousness of entire
insulation from his species, none of that awe
which is inspired by those terrific outlines which
display the convulsions of nature or threaten
the existence of the beholder. It is impossible
to gaze on the fertile hills and rich bottoms
that extend on either side, without fancying
them peopled ; and even where no signs of population appear, the imagination is continually
reaching forward to the period when these
luxuriant spots shall maintain their millions.

The absence of population alluded to, is to
be considered in a comparative sense. With
Ohio on the one hand, Kentucky and Virginia
on the other, there can be no dearth of inhabitants; but their dwellings are less frequently
presented to the traveller's eye than might be
supposed. Every day we pass villages, great or
small, and farm houses are scattered along the
shore ; but we often float for miles without discovering any indication of the residence of
human beings. Many of the river bottoms are
inundated annually, and land has not yet become
so scarce or valuable as to induce the owners to

reclaim these spots from the dominion of the water. Such places remain covered with gigantic timber, which conceals the habitations beyond them. The commanding eminences are seldom occupied, because the settlers are farmers, who consult convenience, rather than beauty, in the location of their dwellings, and who generally pitch their tents in the vicinity of a spring, upon the low grounds.

The beautiful islands, which are numerous, should not be forgotten. These are sometimes large and fertile, but generally inundated. and seldom under cultivation. Sometimes they are mere sandbanks, covered with thick groves of the melancholy willow, whose branches dip into the water.

For several days after leaving Cincinnatti, our progress was delayed by bad weather. We have had a series of what are called *April days*; why they are so called I know not, for April, bating the sins and fooleries of her first day, is as inoffensive a month as any in the calendar. The high winds have frequently obliged us to stop, and tie our boat to the bushes, under whose shelter we have remained beating,

N

against the shore for hours together; while the rain has as often driven us from the deck. Thunder and lightning, sunshine, rain, and wind, have succeeded each other as rapidly as the changing scenes and mimic tempests of the play-house. If I were an *English traveller,* I should consider myself fully authorised, under these circumstances, to note down, that " the climate of this country is dreadfully tempestuous, and the waves of the Ohio as boisterous as those of the Gulph Stream;" but as the wind sometimes blows on the coasts of the Atlantic, and the rain sometimes falls in England, I am rather inclined to think that as an *American traveller,* it is safest not to notice this as a peculiarity— for, in the latter character, it will be expected of me that I shall tell the truth, though the former would not have imposed any such obligation.

We all know the difficulty of disposing of a rainy day. How the worthy patriarch Noah contrived to make use of forty of them in succession, I cannot imagine, unless it were in receiving and entertaining the numerous guests who solicited his hospitality during that period, for *one* has always sufficed to exhaust my

patience. But of all irksome places of confinement in a rainy day, deliver me from a keel-
boat. Had I the good fortune to be one of
those geological or chymical gentry, who write
such vastly learned books, I should turn these
freaks of the weather to fine account, I promise
you. It would be an ill wind indeed that
should not blow me some good. Every zephyr
should whisper me a new theory—every thunder cloud furnish materials for a chapter.
Never was there such a theatre for a lover of
science as is displayed in this new country.
The soil which the hand of man has not yet
spoiled teems with productions, which in older
countries are laboriously sought and seldom
found. The atmosphere has many peculiarities
which are yet to be examined and explained.
Volney declares that " the excessive heats of
summer," (in the western country) " bring
with them almost *daily* storms," and it has been
asserted that not only every man, woman, and
child, but every ox, hog, and even squirrel,
has *the liver complaint.* Thus, instead of plunder-
ing graves for human bodies, the anatomist
might find a *subject* on every tree, and could

innocently trace the secretion of bile in the
liver of the squirrel. Here is "ample room
and verge enough" for the professors of all the
ologies, unless it be craniology—for skulls are
not over abundant hereabout, and they are held
in such respect by their owners, that he who
should examine them too curiously might
chance to get his own broken. But I have no
taste for these *grave* sciences, and am at best
but a lazy traveller. I should never be able to
endure the drudgery of travelling with an apparatus of microscopes, crucibles, thermometers,
and quadrants—to say nothing of maps, com-
mon-place books, and writing materials. I love
Nature, as in duty bound, and am sincerely
grateful for the many good and agreeable
things, she is kind enough to furnish. I admire
her too, and delight to gaze upon her beauties.
I contemplate them as I do those of a lovely
female, without the least curiosity to pry into
matters which lie beyond the surface. But as
I disdain the sciences, let me pass on to my
narrative.

In the early part of our voyage, we overtook
a flat boat floating down the stream, and in

passing were hailed by a person on the roof,
who was no sooner recognized by our boatmen
than a murmur of joy ran throughout the boat.
In a few minutes the stranger came on board,
and was received with a hearty welcome by our
men, who saluted him by the title of " Pappy."
He seemed to be about fifty years of age, but
the hand of time had passed so lightly over him
as to have left but little impression; hard
labour and exposure had operated more power-
fully than the years which had rolled over his
head; for the sallow hue of his complexion, and
the frosty tinge of his hair, were strongly con-
trasted with the robust activity of his limbs.
His eye had all the fire, and his step the elas-
ticity, of youth; a continual smile lurked among
his sly features, and the jest was ever on his
lips; while an affected gravity, a drawling
accent, and a kind, benevolent manner, which
accorded well with the paternal appellation
given him by the boatmen, marked him as an
eccentric being. In every walk of life we find
privileged characters, who consider themselves above the ordinary rules which regulate
social intercourse; and although such persons

differ widely from each other, each assumes within his respective sphere a powerful influence over less original minds. Our "Pappy" was a humourist of this description, and his sway among his fellow boatmen was unlimited. To the great joy of the crew, he was hired for the trip, and hastened back to the flat, to bring as he expressed it "Katy and his plunder on board." Katy, whose merry voice we soon heard, was no other than a violin, and his *plunder* consisted of a small parcel of clothing tied up in a bandanna handkerchief. It was I suppose his all—had it been less, "Old Pap" would still have been merry; if it had been infinitely greater, he would still have joked and fiddled. This veteran boatman had not seen half a century, without his share of those afflictions which embitter life ; he had tasted deeply, as I understood, the cup of domestic misery, but it had not saddened nor soured his temper. He was a man of endless humour—a fellow of infinite fancy. While others worked, he would sit for hours scraping upon his violin, singing catches, or relating merry and marvellous tales. When he chose to labour he went to the oar,

when inclined to trifle he did so, and no one
questioned his motions, but, whether at play or
at work, he applied himself with all his heart. If
the boat grounded on a sand-bar, he was the
first to plunge into the water ; if a point was to
be weathered, or a rapid to be passed, his was
always the best oar ; if a watch was to be kept
at night, who so wakeful as he ? And on such
occasions, he would fiddle and sing the live-long
night. In short, with the affectation, and somewhat of the appearance of age, he was the
gayest, most active, and stoutest man on board ;
and I was told that there were but few men
along the river, who would have undertaken to
handle " Old Pap."

This new recruit proved a great acquisition,
for, like all other merry men, he was the cause of
merriment in others. He kept our own crew in
good humour, and hailed every boat we passed
with some stroke of pleasantry. More than
once he enacted chief musician at dances got
up at the hovels along shore, near which we *lay
by* for the night. Lady Morgan styles this
amusement the " poetry of motion," and I assure
you it was not the less poetic with the accompaniment of Pap and his musical Kate.

LETTER XII.

THE FALLS OF OHIO—SCENERY AND PRODUCTIONS BELOW THE FALLS.

On the 28th of April, we arrived at Louisville, at the Falls of the Ohio, and landed at Bear-grass Creek, above the town. Boats usually stop here to take in a pilot, without which it is unsafe to descend the rapids. I remained but a few hours—strolled through the streets—saw some very fine houses, and some very busy people—eat an excellent dinner at Allen's Hotel—took a hack and rode to Shipping-sport, where I visited several fine steamboats, and returned. I was pleased with what I saw, but saw too little to justify any comment.

It is worth a voyage down the Ohio to pass the rapids. They are two miles in length, with a descent of twenty-two feet and a half in that distance, and are formed by ledges of rock, which extend quite across the river. The current is said to have an average velocity of thirteen miles an hour, which of course is increased or diminished by high or low water.

To the voyager who is about to venture into this headlong current, three *roads* are presented ; the Indian *Chute*, which is not passable in low water, the Kentucky *Chute*, which is only passable in high water, and the Middle *Chute* which at any time is the best. The word *Chute** may puzzle you as much as it has puzzled me ; but it is the very identical word used by most of the writers on this subject. Whether it be a Greek, an Indian, or a Kentucky phrase, I cannot inform you—I have sought its derivation in all the languages with which I am conversant, without effect. In point of fact, it is applied to channels through which a boat may be said to *shoot* with the swiftness of an arrow.

As you approach the head of the rapids, the mighty stream rolls on in a smooth unbroken

* Had the author consulted the French dictionary, he would have seen that the word *chute* is Anglice *fall*. Perhaps the Americans may never yet have heard of a *parachute*—Anglice, to prevent a fall.

sheet, increasing in velocity as you advance.
The business of preparation creates a sense of
impending danger : the pilot, stationed on the
deck, assumes command ; a firm and skilful
helmsman guides the boat; the oars, strongly
manned, are vigorously plied to give the vessel
a *momentum* greater than that of the current,
without which the helm would be inefficient.
The utmost silence prevails among the crew ;
but the ear is stunned with the sound of rushing waters : and the sight of waves dashing, and
foaming, and whirling among the rocks and
eddies below, is grand and fearful.   The boat
advances with inconceivable rapidity to the
head of the channel—" takes the *Chute*"—and
seems no longer manageable among the angry
currents, whose foam dashes upon her deck,
but in a few moments she emerges from their
power, and rides again in serene waters.

No incident worthy of remark occurred for
several days.   One morning about sun-rise
I had just risen, when I heard one of the boatmen make some observation about an *elegant
smell*, and as I love to *see* elegant things, I
hastened to the deck.   The air was filled with

delightful odours, emanating from the wild grape-vines, then in bloom, mingled perhaps with the sweets from other blossoms. I had heard the word *elegant* so often misused in this country, that I was not surprised at this singular application of it. The good folks here have elegant hogs, and elegant bacon, elegant corn, and elegant whiskey, elegant land, and elegant tobacco; we have a man on board who is said to be an "elegant oarsman," another who is an "elegant hand with an axe," while *Old Pap* and Katy discourse "most elegant music."

As I have not attempted any thing like a regular journal, 1 shall pass on at once as far as the mouth of Green River, which we passed on the 3rd of May.

Here we find a country essentially different from that above the Falls. Changes have been gradually presented to the eye as we advanced, which are now sufficiently developed to indicate an essential difference of country, soil, and climate. The country is flat, the soil deep, black, and rich. Small ranges of hills are seen at intervals. The river bottoms become more extensive, exhibit decided appearances of annual inundation, and are intersected by *bayoux*, or deep inlets, which are channels for the water in time of flood, and remain empty during the rest of the year. *Cane-brakes* are occasionally seen along the banks. The cane is an evergreen, from twelve to twenty feet in height, which grows only in rich wet flats. It stands so thick upon the ground, as to form an almost impenetrable thicket, and as it is usually found among ponds and *bayoux*, the *cane-brake* is always a secure retreat for *bears*, which feed upon the buds, and for deer and other gregarious animals. The first settlers find them very valuable, as affording food for their cattle during the winter ; and even after the country has been many years settled, the inhabitants drive their cattle *to the cane* in the autumn, and suffer them to remain without any further attention until the ensuing spring. The cane, however, is generally destroyed in a few years, by the large number of cattle which are thus wintered upon it. Cattle and horses eat it greedily, and will stray several miles in search of this favourite food, which is said to be very nourishing.

Cotton-wood, peccans, catalpas, and gigantic

sycamores, are now seen in the rich bottoms. Extensive groves of cotton-wood are sometimes seen. The tree is large and extremely tall; the foliage of a rich deep green, resembling that of the *Lombardy poplar*, to which tree this also assimilates somewhat in shape. Nothing can exceed the beauty of these groves: at a distance, a stranger might imagine them forests of Lombardy poplar; and as that tree is devoted to ornamental purposes, it is scarcely possible to refrain from fancying, that some splendid mansion is concealed in the impervious shade; while the deep gloom with which they envelop the soil, gives a wild, pensive, and solemn character to the *cotton-tree grove*.

The catalpa is a small graceful tree, remarkable for the beauty of its flowers. The peccan is a tall tree, resembling the hickory, to which, if naturalists speak truly, it is nearly related; it yields a rich, fine nut, of which large quantities are annually exported. Grape-vines are numerous and very large, the stems being sometimes nearly a foot in thickness, though seldom exceeding six or eight inches, and the branches extending to the tops of the tallest trees.

The misletoe begins to be seen among the branches of the large trees. This little plant never grows upon the ground, but with a very poetic taste, takes up its attic residence upon the highest limbs. The berry which contains the seed is so viscous as to adhere to the feet of birds, who carry it from tree to tree, and thus contribute to its propagation.

Here too large flocks of paroquets are heard chattering in the woods, or seen sporting their bright green plumage in the sun-beams.

On the 4th of May a violent wind again forced us to seek shelter under the shore. We landed at the mouth of a small creek in Indiana. Here we found a fine rich bottom, lying higher than those we have passed, and but little of which has been overflowed. The forest was thick and tangled, and so choked with the trunks of fallen trees, weeds, and brush, as to be almost inaccessible. So fertile is the soil that every spot produces something. We penetrated a short distance into the brake, and saw several deer, and a number of turkeys. At the foot of a large tree we discovered a quantity of the hair of a wild cat; we found many places where fires had been kindled, probably by hunters, who no doubt frequently visit this solitary spot, which appears to abound in game. Immediately below us is a *clearing* which seems to have been made some years ago, and near it another of more recent origin. On a rising spot is a log house, in a state of dilapidation, and the ruins of another but a few rods distant, which has been burned.

The situation is so beautiful, and the land so exceedingly rich, that I could not help speculating upon the probable cause which had driven away the occupant of this romantic spot. A few years ago we might have attributed its evacuation to the tomahawk and fire-brand of the Indian. Indeed, the poet who wished to sketch the deserted cabin of a murdered woodsman, could not select a more appropriate scene. The ruined cabins, the rank weeds around them, the embers in the wood, the tangled brake, the wild luxuriance of the soil and herbage, with the stillness of the gloomy shades, would afford rich materials for a lively imagination. But as the yell of the hostile Indian has long ceased to be heard in this direction, we must suppose that sickness or misfortune (or both,) has visited with a rude hand the late tenant of these shadowy wilds.

On the 6th of May, I arrived at Shawnee Town, in Illinois, and bade adieu to the keel-boat.

LETTER XIII.

NAMES OF PLACES.

In passing down the Ohio, and indeed in every part of America, the traveller is amused with the singular and various tastes displayed in the names of places. It would seem that our worthy countrymen had but little regard for the tender sensibilities of future generations, whose inheritance they have patched and spangled with the shreds and remnants of every age and country. We have been supplied

" By saint, by savage, and by sage;"

Europe, Asia, and Africa, have been ransacked, and we have culled all the fields of literature,

o

sacred, classic, and profane. The tourist
passes in a twinkling, from Troy to Siberia,
from Rome to Calcutta, from Vienna to Car-
thage, from Herculaneum to Petersburgh ; and
if he chooses to continue his jaunt, he may
visit every part of the globe almost as rapidly
as the sun himself. But if he be a poet, or an
antiquary, he must not be too sanguine in his
expectations : for these places have no arche-
types in the old world. He may freeze to
death in the very centre of our Vesuvius, and
perspire at every pore at the view of Kamts-
chatka. There is no Pantheon at the modern
Rome, and no Pagoda in the new Hindostan.
He will find no splendid ruins at Palmyra, nor
hallowed sepulchres in Palestine. In Goshen
he will see Yankees from the " land of steady
habits," instead of captive Israelites ; and
where he might expect an extensive manufactory of bricks, he will find a land abounding in
cheese and timberclocks. We adhere to old
names with a wonderful pertinacity, although
destitute of the characteristics with which
those names are associated. The dearest
places in some of our towns are called *Cheap-*

side, and insects are never sold in the *Fly-Market.* In this particular, we resemble some worthy families, who hand down a favourite baptismal name from generation to generation, although the dandy Jeremiah of to-day may have little in common with him who lamented over the sins of the Hebrews, and as little with the honest ancestor who first bequeathed the appellation to his unborn descendants.

I confess I am not pleased with the dearth of invention indicated by the adoption of these exotics; and am the less so, when I observe the admirable taste displayed in those which are of domestic manufacture. These are fraught with meaning, and generally allude to some historical fact or local peculiarity. If any of the early navigators of these rivers saw an otter, a fox, or a bear on the shore, they were sure to name the nearest creek or island after that animal. If an individual sickened or died, the catastrophe was perpetuated in the same manner. The appellations thus casually given, are retained when the *per quod* upon which they were founded has failed or is forgotten. Thus we now find a Pigeon-Creek,

o 2

where there are no pigeons, and a Crow Island where there is no carrion. As to the taste displayed in them, you have only to imagine them ranged in the lines of some future poet, who may fancy to waft his heroine down *the beautiful stream.* How delightfully would such names as *Horsetail Ripple*, Dead Man's Island, Hog Island, Big Seweekly, Loggstown, Crow's Island, Big Beaver, Raccoon Creek, Custard Island, Big Yellow, Mingo Bottom Island, White Woman, and Opossum Creek, jingle in verse! How admirably would they set off the peculiar style of Sir Walter Scott! Even so humble a poet as myself might render a humble incident poetic, with the aid of such harmonious epithets ;—for instance :—

> O'er *Horsetail* when the stream was low,
> Waded a bold misguided cow ;
> False *Horsetail !* caverns lurk below
>   Thy wave, that glitters joyously !

> Soon *Horsetail* heard a dreadful sound ;
> *Dead Man* and *Big Seweekly* groaned ;
> *Raccoon* and *Little Beaver* moaned ;
>   And *'Possum* joined the symphony.

White Woman heard, and whiter grew;
Big Yellow almost turned to blue;
Altered, sweet *Custard*, was thy hue,
Sad *Brindle* low'd so piteously.

Gallant *Hog Island*, it was thine
From death to save the bellowing kine,
As Jaffier from the " envious" brine,
Snatch'd lovely Belvidera.

" St. Louis," says Mr. Breckenridge, " was formerly called *Pain Court*, (short bread), from the privations of the first settlers." The French have left some curious names in Missouri, where we find *La Femme Osage*, (the Osage woman); *Misère*, (Misery); *Crève Cœur*, (Broken Heart); *Vuide Poche*, (Empty Pocket); *Bon Homme* (Good Man); *La Rivière des Pères*, (the River of Fathers); *La Rivière au Vase*, (the River of Mud); *Bois Brulé*, (Burnt Wood, pronounced by the Americans, *Bob Ruby*); *Côte sans Dessein*, which you may translate for yourself: I should call it *Accidental Hill*, which is justified by the appearance of the place. It is an eminence on a hill, without a valley, and which looks as if it did not belong to the place, but had been dropped by accident. Some of these names are now discarded, and the people would be quite scandalized at their revival—like the good citizens of a flourishing town in Pennsylvania, which was formerly called *Cat-fish Camp*, but where a man would now be almost *tarred and feathered*, for mentioning a *cat-fish*.

Many of the French names in this country have been corrupted. The upper part of the Kaskaskia River is called by a name which is spelt so variously that I can hardly undertake to write it. The literal pronunciation is *O-kaw*, but it is written by travellers and others Occoa, Oka, Ocra, &c. As this stream is in fact the Kaskaskia, and was probably taken by the first French explorist for a *branch* of that river, it is probable that, contracting the name of the latter, they called it *Au Kas ;* this reading accords with the practice of that people, who frequently use abbreviations : thus Kaskaskia is called *Kas-kee*, and Cahokia, *Caho*. So, if you ask a Frenchman where he is going, he will answer " *Au Post*," to the Post, meaning the post of Vincennes. This being the principal fortress in this country, previous to its settlement, was for a long while called *The Post ;* and from the

French mode of expression, *Au Post!* it acquired among the first American settlers the name *O-Pose*, by which it is still commonly known.

There is a small stream in Illinois called *Bonpas*. The author of a book of " Geographical Sketches," writes *Bumpaw*, and his orthography is adopted by many persons; the original name must have been *Bonne Passe*, (a good channel), though in fact it can hardly be said to have any channel.

There was an Indian chief in some of the southern territories, so noted for his vigilance that he was said by his followers to " sleep with one eye ;" in consequence of which the French termed him *Dor d'un Œil*, and bestowed the same appellation upon a small creek which watered his hunting grounds. The Americans adopted the sense, and as nearly as they could, the sound of this significant cognomen, and the creek is still called *Dordon Eye*.

The term " Lost Creek" occurs to the traveller so frequently as to excite his curiosity. Poets, indeed, have been liberal in bestowing attributes upon the limpid stream, which is said to babble and to murmur, to creep slug-

gishly along, or to "hold its way rejoicing."
There is even morality in water-courses, and
one bard discovers " books in the running
brooks." But though brooks run, and even
wander and stray, no one ever heard until now
of their getting lost. Yet it seems that this accident sometimes befalls them. In a level, woody
country, where the soil is rich and deep, a small
stream sometimes spreads by innumerable small
channels over a vast surface, until its distinctive
character is lost in swamps and puddles; a
creek which falls into this dilemma is sure to be
dubbed " Lost Creek." Woe to the traveller
who finds this name upon the road before him—
dismal swamps and miry paths await him.

The word *country* is used by our people in a
manner peculiar to themselves. When we say
" this country," we do not mean North America, nor the United States, nor any state, but
a particular section of country, frequently of
indefinite extent. Thus that part of Kentucky
which lies south of Green River is called the
Green River Country; a part of Illinois, lying
upon the Sangamon River, is called the *Sangamon
Country;* the province of Texas is called the

Texas Country ; and a part of the State of New York used to be called (and may be yet) the *Genessee Country.* The phrase is arbitrary and fluctuating—sometimes applied to a state, and sometimes to a part of a state—now to a country, and at other times to several countries. It is applied to a large region, when that region is unsettled, or has not yet been divided into districts or counties, or when those divisions are little known, and the names of them not in familiar use. What was lately called the *Alabama Country,* is now the State of Alabama, and the *Red River Country* will soon be divided between Texas and Arkansas.

The people of Illinois have called the metropolis of their state Vandalia. As this designation was given by the commissioners who selected this spot for the seat of government, not a little surprise was excited that they should have chosen so barbarous an appellation. It is said, that while they were in solemn deliberation on this point, and in great perplexity to find a name for their infant city, a facetious gentleman, who happened to be present, informed them, that there had been a tribe of *Indians* who existed many centuries ago, among the forests and prairies which now form the fairest portion of this state, who were called *Vandals*. There was also a contemporary tribe called Goths. Whether these rival nations had fought like the two Kilkenny cats, who devoured each other until nothing was left of either *but the tips of the tails*, the learned gentleman did not state; but the name of *Vandalia* was adopted in honour of the aborigines. This story has probably more wit than truth in it. It is also said, that this place was called after a Frenchman, one of the first whites who penetrated these forests, who resided for many years near this spot, and was famous as an expert hunter and a daring foe to his Indian neighbours.

There is a branch of the Little Wabash River in Illinois, called the *Skillet Fork*, which took its name from the following circumstance. During the late war, companies of rangers (a kind of mounted militia) were ordered out to protect the western frontiers from the Indians; a detachment of these troops, under the command of Colonel Willis Hargrave, now a Major General of Militia in this state, having fallen

upon the track of some Indians, pursued them
to the banks of this stream, where they lost
the track—the Indians having taken to the
water. It was necessary to cross over to continue the chase ; but the stream, swelled with
rains, roared like a torrent, and the shores were
so abrupt that it was impossible to plunge the
horses in with their riders, and if they could
even have reached the opposite bank, it would
have been impracticable to ascend it. Such
obstacles are easily surmounted by backwoodsmen, unused to ferries and bridges. The men
were soon employed in constructing rafts to
carry them over ; one headstrong fellow, named
Smith, dashed forward—reached the edge of
the bank—plunged in—and horse and rider disappeared. In a moment Smith was seen swimming in one direction, and his horse in another,
both dashing the waves aside, " with hearts of
controversy ;" both reached the land in safety,
but with the loss of the baggage. The party
soon crossed, but a sad discovery awaited them :
they were divided into *messes,* and one man was
appointed, each day, in every *mess,* to cook the
victuals and carry the culinary utensils. Smith

held the important office of cook on that event-
ful day, and when they encamped in the evening it was discovered that his mess were not
only destitute of provisions, but had lost what
was of infinitely more importance, a *skillet*
which composed the whole apparatus of their
kitchen ; the " envious wave" had robbed him
of skillet, bread, bear-meat and all. Here was
a dilemma ! a woful dilemma, which none but
Indian hunters can appreciate. Bread could
not be procured in the woods, and game they
dared not shoot, for fear of alarming the foe,
whose footsteps they were silently tracking. But
if Providence had showered *manna* in their path,
or their own cunning ensnared the " dappled
denizen of the forest," of what avail would it
have been ? They had no skillet wherein to
dress it ! The vexation of the *mess*, the cha-
grin of Smith, and the jests of their comrades,
kept the affair alive in their memories for a
long while, and the stream which caused this
dire mishap is still called the *Skillet Fork*.

Another creek in this state, was named by
the same party. They were lying on its
banks round a fire, at night, when some of the

company undertook to practise a joke upon
Smith.   A sappling was bent to the ground, to
which they tied his heels as he slept, and on
letting it go he was swung aloft.   His cries
roused the whole party, who, imagining the
Indians were at hand, flew to their posts, nor
was the alarm dispelled, until the unlucky cause
of it was discovered dangling in the air.   The
stream was called *Smith's Fork*, and still retains
the name.

About twelve or fourteen years ago, a gentleman named Rector, a brother of the late Surveyor
General, was travelling from St. Louis to Shawnee
Town, when he fell into an ambuscade of hostile
Indians, within twenty miles of the latter place.
He was not aware of his danger until he saw
himself surrounded by the foe, and heard the
appalling war-whoop of the painted warriors,
who issued, like the followers of Roderick Dhu,
from every shade.   Directly in the path, but a
few paces before him, stood a savage, who, as he
discharged his rifle, laughed loud with a diabol-
ical expression of malignant triumph, as if
sure of his victim.   The ball passed through
Rector's body, who still retained sufficient

presence of mind to endeavour to escape.
The path which he travelled was completely
closed behind him; before him was a deep miry
creek, whose high perpendicular banks overhanging the channel, seemed to render a passage
impossible at any place but the ford to which
he had been hastening, and the path to which
was occupied by the enemy. He could only
give the rein and the spur to his horse, and
trust to Providence. The gallant steed, who
was also badly wounded, quitting the path,
rushed to the bank of the stream, and with a
desperate leap, plunged to the bottom, and
extricating himself from the mire, ascended the
steep bank on the opposite side, and soon bore
his master, now entirely insensible, beyond the
reach of danger. The Indians, fearing pursuit,
fled in contrary directions. The unconscious
Rector kept his seat for several miles, while
the noble horse, as if tender of his charge, carried him safely through the thick and bushy
forest. At length Rector fell, but the horse
continued to fly at full speed until he reached
the Saline, about six miles from the scene of
the disaster. Here a few persons resided,

engaged in making salt; to whom the bleeding
wounds of the horse readily conveyed the intelligence of what had happened; but they
were too few to oppose the enemy, nor did
they dare to leave their families exposed.   One
of them was sent express to Shawnee Town,
who quickly returned with a party of eight or
ten men.   These, reinforced by the people at
the Saline, pursued the track of the horse, who
was readily traced through the snow, which lay
deep on the ground.   They found Rector,
cold, stiff, and apparently dead : a rifle ball had
passed through his breast.   Happily one of the
party was a physician, through whose care and
skill the sufferer was resuscitated, and eventually
recovered.   Leaving a few of their party with
the wounded man, the remainder proceeded to
the scene of action.   Here they found the
tracks of a considerable number of Indians ;
they traced the horse from the path to the
edge of the bank ; they saw where he had leaped
down a descent of about *twenty* feet to the
surface of the water, had broken through the
ice in the middle of the creek, and had clamber-
ed up an almost perpendicular bank on the

other side.   Had not the new fallen-snow, the
tracks of the horse's feet, and the blood-drops
which marked his whole course, rendered all
this as plain as demonstration, those who then
stood upon the margin of the rivulet would
have thought it impossible for a horse to effect a
passage at that spot; yet Rector's horse accomplished it, bearing a heavy burthen, and himself
wounded in a vital part.   One of the balls
received by this fine animal passed through
his breast immediately behind the shoulders.
Several of those who inspected him, who had
been accustomed to hunting all their lives, and
were well acquainted with the formation of
quadrupeds, and the effect of gun-shot wounds,
have assured me that nine out of ten would
have died instantly of such a wound ; yet the
horse recovered to entire health, and was cherished during life with the tenderest care, by
his grateful master.   The Indians were pursued
for a considerable distance, but not overtaken.
This stream, which empties itself into the Saline
River, is called *Rector's Fork*.

You will perceive that where two streams
unite, the lesser is frequently termed *a fork* of

the larger into which it empties, as the *North Fork of the Saline*, the *Skillet Fork of Little Wabash, Smith's Fork of Muddy.*

Many of the old names in this country have been anglicised, though not often judiciously. The name of the town in which for the present I have fixed my " local habitation," has suffered a very disadvantageous change. The Indian word Sha-wa-noe was not inharmonious, but it has been corrupted into Shawnee Town. A stream which the French called *la Rivière au Vase* is transformed into *Muddy ;* but as there happens to be two of the same name, they are called Big and Little Muddy. The practice of giving the same name to two neighbouring streams, and distinguishing one of them by the classic word *big*, is very common. We have Big and Little Wabash, Big and Little Miami, Big and Little Beaver, and I suppose a hundred other such ill sorted pairs, who seem not to be united under any canon of the church, or rule of taste. I once travelled through Illinois when the waters were high ; and when I was told that *Little Mary* would stop me, and that to get by *Big Mary* was impossible, I supposed them to

P

be attractive damsels, who, like beauteous Circe
of old, amused themselves with playing *tricks
upon travellers.* But lo! instead of blushing,
blooming, and melodious maids, I found torrents cold as ice, and boisterous as furies.
Mary is too sweet a name to be thus profaned.

There are some sentimental names, which
should not be forgotten—some sweet-sounding
epithets, which recal the joys of Arcadia.
Such are Corydon, Feliciana, Cynthiana, and
divers others, equally tender and appropriate.

We have another cognomen peculiar to the
West, which is conveyed in the beautiful word
Lick. We have *Salt Licks, Blue Licks, Sulphur
Licks, Big Bone Licks,* and *Licks* of all sorts
and sizes. The word is uncouth enough, but
is very descriptive, and designates those spots
which have been frequented by wild grazing
animals, for the purpose of *licking* the saline
particles with which the earth is impregnated.
Some of these places have been *licked* for centuries, until vast cavities have been formed in
the surface of the ground. By these appearances the early settlers were directed to many
valuable minerals. But surely this barbarous

appellative might be dropped now, when the aboriginal *lickers* have been expelled, and these places converted into valuable manufactories, and polite watering-places.

An extensive *genus* of names is derived from our patriotic ancestors, and from living characters of celebrity. The western people have displayed an honourable feeling in thus perpetuating the memories of distinguished men. In Kentucky, out of seventy-one counties, all are called after eminent men but *eight*. Ohio, in 1819, had fifty counties, of which thirty were called after individuals, ten have Indian names, and one is called *Licking*. In Illinois and Indiana, all the counties are named in the same manner, except two in each state. A large number of towns are also named after patriots and heroes. From this laudable custom, a serious inconvenience arises in the frequent repetition of the same name ; an evil which is aggravated by a foolish propensity of emigrants for naming the place at which they settle in honour of that which they have left. We have now in the United States about twenty Salems ; we have Fairfields, Clearfields, and

Middletowns, without number. The Washingtons, Waynes, and Jeffersons, baffle calculation.

The seat of Government of Missouri is to be removed to *Cote sans Dessein*, which, it is said, is to assume the name of *Missouriopolis.* Indiana has called her capital *Indianopolis;* and it is to be hoped, that Arkansas will adopt Arkopolis ; for such is the passion for imitation, that a name no sooner gets into genteel use, than it goes the rounds.

Thus I have written you a long letter on a very scientific subject, and which, if our country was a thousand years older, might make me a fellow of a philosophical society. But, alas! we know our origin so well, that there is no chance of passing for an antiquary now-a-days—unless indeed we delve into Indian lore, an unprofitable field! for the wisest of those who explore it are unable to determine whether our copper-coloured brethren are Jews, Kamschatkadales, or Welshmen. The subject, however, of which I have treated is not without interest. Older nations know nothing of the origin or meaning of half the names which occur on their maps, and many a solitary midnight lamp has in vain lent its rays to develop the obscurity. A mysterious appellation, supposed to be fraught with meaning, has often been chased with unavailing assiduity, through labyrinths of parchment and black letter, and finally lost among the mists of tradition—which, if discovered, might be found to be as frivolous in its application, as some of those which I have explained. No other nation has had the opportunity which we enjoy, of forming its own geographical vocabulary. They have been indebted to accident, or to the rude conceptions of the nations who preceded them, for that which among us is to be the fruit of our own taste. Nations are continually rising to power, or declining into imbecility, and their rise or fall is a continual lesson, fraught with instruction. In these changes every institution bears a part, and therefore should the progress of every institution, however trifling, which forms an integral part of national character or wealth, be observed. A Latin poet has said, *stultus labor est ineptiarum*, and I am not disposed to controvert the maxim ; for I do not consider that employment trifling, which may add a mite to the literature of my country or to the amusement of my friends. For them I shall always be proud to toil, though sober-sided Gravity may shake his head, and his friend the critic pronounce my exertions *labor ineptiarum.*

LETTER XIV.

SHAWNEE TOWN AND ITS VICINITY.

No place in the western country has been more vilified than Shawnee Town. The slang which English travellers adopt in relation to every thing American, has been used even by our countrymen in relation to this place. If the former only had depreciated its local and moral character, its inhabitants might be satisfied; for, accustomed as Englishmen are to sneer at all that is respectable in our institutions, or attractive in our natural or political history, all, in short, that evinces the superiority of a young, vigorous, and virtuous country, over the vicious decrepitude of " the fast anchored isle," their censure is the best praise that could be extorted from their lips. The present race of *Shawanoese* have indeed been depicted as

being in no wise superior to their savage predecessors : nor could the picture drawn of them
have been much aggravated by adding the
crimes of Sodom and the plagues of Egypt. A
few years ago, the traveller, when he arrived
here, loosened the hilt of his dirk, and prepared
to gallop through as fast as possible, fully convinced that every moment was fraught with
peril ; he fancied that if he should be so fortunate as not to fall into the hands of the *natives*,
he had still to apprehend the danger of having
his joints racked with the ague, and all the
blood in his veins sucked out by the musquitoes.
There is one advantage at least, in a credulous
disposition, that it always furnishes an ample
harvest of the marvellous to those whose want
of intellect disables them from gathering amusement from other sources.

It would be tedious to cite all the authors
who have disseminated such nonsense. Gentlemen who travel, and write their travels, too
often imitate the conduct of a certain English
tourist, who, on arriving at a town in Europe,
where he was received by a red-haired landlord
and a drunken landlady, noted in his common-

place book, " all the men in Alsace are red-haired, and the women get drunk." It would be useless to attempt to reclaim such licentious tourists ; we might as well " whistle jigs to a mile-stone" as expostulate with those who thus sin against light and knowledge. But we can expose them.

A writer of a book of " Geographical Sketches *on* the Western country," published at Cincinnatti in 1819, comprises all his knowledge of Shawnee Town in the following brief paragraph : "Shawnee Town, eight miles below the Wabash, on the Ohio, is subject to inundation by high water. It is the place where courts of justice are held for Gallatin County. It contains a bank called the *Great Bank of Illinois*, with a capital of two millions of dollars, and a land office for the district." The writer of this would have conferred a singular favour upon the inhabitants of Shawnee Town, if he had been good enough to designate exactly the street, lane, or alley, upon which this *Great Bank* is situated, as the oldest inhabitants have no recollection of any such institution. In the present scarcity of money such a bank would be much resorted to

for loans, and out of *two millions* must no doubt
have several odd hundreds of thousands of idle
specie, the emission of which would be highly
beneficial. It is hoped that the author will
furnish the desired information on this point, in
his next edition of " Sketches *on* the Western
Country," and that he will style this mammoth
nstitution the *Father Bank of the West*, in opposition to the *Mother Bank* at Philadelphia.
There is a little bank here, with a capital of three
hundred thousand dollars, which has been in
operation eight or nine years, and amid the wreck
of credit and the crush of banks, has always
paid specie for its notes, and retained the
public confidence.   But as this is a mere
chicken compared with the Colossus above
mentioned, it cannot be supposed to be the one
alluded to.

   The following account of the same place is extracted from " The Navigator :"—" It possesses
about thirty indifferent cabin-roofed houses,
with the exception of one or two that are
shingled. It has a post-office, two or three indifferent taverns, and several dram-shops. The
U. S. saline salt works being near this place,

they give employment and afford a source of trade to such of the inhabitants as are industrious and enterprising. The town is subject to the inundations of the river ; and during those of the winter and spring of 1813, the inhabitants were obliged to abandon their houses." I will at once concede the praise of general accuracy, and uniform integrity of purpose, to the compiler of this work ; his fault in this instance consists in allowing what was true when it was written, to remain unaltered in subsequent editions, without adverting to the rapid growth of the western towns.

Mr. Birkbeck, with the best of motives, adopts a wonderful mistake. He expresses his surprise that the inhabitants should tenaciously adhere to a spot, from which they are *annually* driven by inundation, and forced to take refuge on the hills.

The Quarterly Review says, "A dirk is the constant companion of every gentleman in Illinois," which of course includes the good people of Shawnee. Rejecting all these accounts, I will give you that which I believe to be correct.

Shawnee Town occupies a beautiful situation on the western bank of the Ohio, nine miles below the mouth of the Wabash, and one hundred and twenty miles above the junction of the Ohio and Mississippi. Its distance from Pittsburgh, by water, is about a thousand miles, and from New Orleans about eleven hundred. The town stands on a level plain, and embraces a view of the river of four or five miles in each direction.

There was formerly a village of Shawnee Indians at this spot, but it was forsaken before the whites attempted a settlement, and no vestige of it now remains but two small mounds. A few cabins were afterwards built by the French traders; but these had also disappeared, and the ground was covered with bushes, when the present town was established. As recently as the year 1808, there was not a house on the ground; in February 1812, an office for the sale of public lands was established at this place; and in March 1814, an act was passed by Congress, providing that two sections of land adjoining Shawnee Town should be laid out into town-lots, streets, avenues, and outlets, and sold in the same manner as other public lands. The town now contains about one hundred houses, of which five or six are of brick, several of frame, and the remainder of log. It has twelve stores, at which a large and active trade is carried on, besides a number of shops of a smaller description; two excellent taverns, an independent bank, and a branch of the state bank; a land office, a post office, two printing offices; and furnishes employment to carpenters, cabinet makers, blacksmiths, tailors, shoemakers, bakers, and other mechanics, of whom a number are settled here.

The ground, as is usually the case in bottom lands, is higher on the edge of the river, where the town stands, than at some distance back, and the town is often insulated, when not actually overflowed. The waters begin to swell in February or March, and continue rising for several weeks. The greatest rise, from the lowest to the highest point, is about fifty feet. The greatest floods of which we have any account, were in 1813 and 1815, when the water covered all the streets, and entered the lower apartments of the dwellings,

reaching nearly to the second floors. Since
that time the inhabitants have not been expelled by the conquering element, although the
water annually covers the plain in the rear of
the town, and advances in front to their very
doors. The inconvenience and alarm occasioned
by the inundations are not so great as might be
supposed. The alarm is little, and that little is
imaginary, because the irruption is not sudden,
nor accompanied with any violent current, or
destructive consequence; and the inconvenience
is temporary, as the waters subside in a few
days, and the soil being sandy, and its surface
uneven, no moisture remains. A small deposit
of decayed vegetable matter is left, but not
enough to corrupt the atmosphere: and even
this, before the weather becomes warm, loses
its deleterious quality by evaporation, or yields
its juices to the vegetable kingdom. When the
river first begins to swell, it usually rises as
much as three or four feet in twenty-four hours;
but as the volume of water increases, its velocity becomes greater, while the widening of the
banks affords it room to expand, and the rise
becomes daily less perceptible. At length it

begins to fill the bayoux, backs up the channels
of the tributary streams, and at last spreads over
the banks, covering the bottoms for miles. This
gradual process affords ample time to the inhabitants to secure their cattle, and to retreat if
necessary. The largest body of water naturally
flows in the deepest channel, and here of course
is the swiftest current, while the shallow waters
which cover the alluvial, flow backwards in
eddies, or have no perceptible motion. For
this reason, dwellings are not *swept away*, and
the inhabitants retreat with safety when the
dwellings are no longer tenable.

Shawnee Town is never overflowed by ordinary floods. To produce this effect a number
of circumstances must concur. All the rivers
which are tributary to the Ohio must swell at
once; and as these are distributed through
Kentucky, Virginia, Pennsylvania, New York,
Ohio, Indiana, and Illinois, there must be a
thaw so general as to melt the snow in all those
states, or rains pervading that whole region.
It has also been remarked, that this town has
never been inundated, except when the *Wabash*
and the Ohio have risen at the same time: an

event which, in the ordinary course of things, can seldom happen, as the sources of these streams are so widely separated that a common cause can seldom affect them both at the same time. It is true, that there is a general similarity of climate throughout all the region watered by the Ohio, and that the approach of spring produces, throughout, the same effect—the melting of snow, the fall of rain, and the rising of rivers.   But these occurrences are accelerated or retarded, in particular places, by slight changes of weather, the fountains are broken up in detail, the waters pass off in succession, and the congregated power of the whole is seldom seen.   Thus. instead of an annual migration, the inhabitants of Shawnee Town have been driven to this expedient but twice.

It might be worthy of inquiry, whether the opening and settling the lands upon the head waters of the tributary streams, will not at some future period decrease the spring floods of the Ohio.   Will not the climate become ameliorated, and the quantity of snow lessened, when the surface of the earth shall be fully exposed to the warmth of the sun?   Will not the accumulation of snow be lessened, by its melting as it falls upon the earth thus exposed? And will not the snow, which now remains buried among the mountains, or in the forests, during the whole winter, and suddenly precipitates itself in immense floods in the spring, be gradually diminished by every gleam of sunshine?

That the low grounds along the margin of the Ohio will be embanked, and the stream confined within its proper channel, as soon as those lands shall acquire a value sufficient to support the expense, cannot be doubted. The Mississippi bottoms have been thus reclaimed, where the volume of water and its perpendicular are both vastly greater than in the Ohio. When this shall be effected, the stream, which is now continually changing its bed, and cutting new channels, will be confined within definite bounds; the body of water will be narrower and deeper; its velocity will be increased; and the force which is now wasted in washing the soil from one bank, and depositing it upon another, will be perpetually exerted in deepening the channel. Many years, perhaps ages, will be

consumed in producing these changes ; but the
consummation must be equally advantageous
to the navigation and to the health of the
country.

The unhealthiness of Shawnee Town has
been assumed as a fact naturally resulting
from its position. But, in point of fact, its inhabitants have been more healthy than those of
any town upon the river, below the falls. As
to musquitoes, they must be admitted to be
quite as numerous as the worst enemies to repose and pleasant dreams could desire,—as
large, as vigorous, and as musical, as any other
musquitoes, grow where they may. We have
heard marvellous tales of the doings of these
pestiferous insects. I forget whether it is Mr.
Weld, or Mr. Ash, or Mr. Moore, who tells
of an audacious musquitoe which bit General
Washington through the *sole of his boot ;* or
which of them it is who relates the tale of a canoe
which was eaten down to the water's edge, by
these ravenous prowlers, who " smelt the blood
of an Englishman," sweating under a load of
blankets within the narrow vessel. I have seen
none quite so large or so malignant as these ;

but I have seen the air filled with them, and
have heard them buzzing the livelong night,
with a noise as loud as that created by a numerous commonwealth of active bees.   There
are two varieties.   The   spring-musquitoe
makes it appearance with the earliest warm
weather, and remains a few weeks, sometimes
only a few days : it is a feeble insect, seldom
biting, and more troublesome to brutes than to
men.   It is most numerous in the woods and
low, wet situations, and seldom appears in the
sunshine ; its most distinctive characteristic is,
that it appears only in the day, while the *fall
musquitoe* is seen only at night.   The latter is
more muscular and sprightly, with a good appetite and sharp teeth ; it is also more dissipated, frolicking all night, and sleeping all day.
It prefers human blood to that of brutes, while
its vernal archetype has a directly opposite taste.
The *fall musquitoe* makes its appearance late
in the summer, and remains until the first frost.
A simple artifice is resorted to for protection
against these marauders — the *musquitoe bar*.
This is a curtain, of the thinnest gauze, or leno,
or some such slight fabric, which admits the

air, and excludes the musquitoe. This is drawn closely round the bed, so as to leave no crevice through which the enemy can enter; and woe to the negligent wight who omits to *tuck in* his *bar;* better endure the stings of conscience, or the freaks of Queen Mab in her worst of humours : no drug nor potion shall " medicine him to that sweet sleep" he knew before.

A remarkable difference occurs in the effect produced by the bite of this insect upon different persons. Natives, or persons *acclimated* by a residence of several years, experience no other inconvenience than instant pain or itching, which subsides immediately, and leaves no vestige. But foreigners are poisoned by the bite ; a slight inflammation ensues, which lasts for several days. I have seen an English lady, not remarkably ugly before, become absolutely hideous in consequence of the vile pimples left by these venomous creatures ; and I knew another, whose feet were so much swollen that she was unable to put on her shoes. But such instances seldom occur, if ever, among the natives or residents.

Before the introduction of steam-boats upon

this river, its immense commerce was chiefly carried on by means of *barges*—large boats, calculated to descend as well as to ascend the stream, and which required many hands to navigate them. Each barge carried from thirty to forty boatmen, and a number of these boats frequently sailed in company. The arrival of such a squadron at a small town was the certain forerunner of riot. The boatmen, proverbially lawless and dissolute, were often more numerous than the citizens, and indulged, without restraint, in every species of debauchery, outrage, and mischief. Wherever vice exists will be found many to abet and to take advantage of its excesses; and these towns were filled with the wretched ministers of crime. Sometimes, the citizens, roused to indignation, attempted to enforce the laws; but the attempt was regarded as a declaration of war, which arrayed the offenders and their allies in hostility; the inhabitants were obliged to unite in the defence of each other, and the contest usually terminated in the success of that party which had least to lose, and were most prodigal of life and careless of consequences.

The rapid emigration to this country was beginning to afford these towns such an increase of population as would have ensured their ascendancy over the despots of the river, when the introduction of steam-boats at once effected a revolution.

The substitution of machinery for manual labour, occasioned a vast diminution in the number of men required for the river navigation. A steam-boat, with the same crew as a barge, will carry ten times the burthen, and perform her voyage in a fifth part of the time required by the latter. The bargemen infested the whole country, by stopping frequently, and often spending their nights on shore; while the steam-boats pass rapidly from one large port to another, making no halt but to receive or discharge merchandise, at intermediate places. The commanders of steam-boats are men of character; property to an immense amount is intrusted to their care; their responsibility is great; and they are careful of their own deportment, and of the conduct of those under their controul. The number of boatmen is therefore not only greatly reduced, in proportion to the amount of trade, but a sort of discipline is introduced among them, while the increase of population has enabled the towns to maintain their police.

During the reign of the bargemen, Shawnee Town, and other places on the river, were described as presenting the most barbarous scenes of outrage, and as being the odious receptacles of every species of filth and villainy. These accounts were probably exaggerated; but that they were true to a certain degree, is readily conceded. But the disorderly character acquired by these towns in the manner I have related, is unjustly attributed to them now, when the fruitful cause of their worst vices has been removed, and when wholesome regulations ensure protection to the peaceable and industrious. Shawnee Town is now a quiet place, exhibiting much of the activity of business, with but little dissipation, and still less of outbreaking disorder.

The Saline Reserve commences a few miles from Shawnee Town, and embraces a tract of ninety thousand acres. There are a number of wells of salt water, the nearest of which is seven and the farthest fourteen miles from town. The Indians resorted to these Salines, for the purpose of making salt, previous to their discovery by the whites ; earthen vessels, of different sizes, used by them in the manufacture, have been found in large numbers by the persons employed in digging wells. Some of these are large, and display no small ingenuity of workmanship ; they are generally fractured ; but one or two have been found entire. Gigantic bones of quadrupeds have also been disinterred, resembling the huge remains which have been dug from the *Licks* in Kentucky. Previous to the erection of the Illinois Territory into a state, the Saline was leased to individuals by the United States ; but at the reception of this state into the Union, this valuable tract was granted to it in perpetuity, with a restriction that it should not be leased at any time for a longer term than ten years. There are now five salt works in operation in the hands of different individuals, at the whole of which an aggregate of immense amount in bushels of salt are manufactured annually, which sells at from thirty-seven and a half to fifty cents a bushel, at the works, or in Shawnee Town. It is sold by weight, the bushel being estimated at sixty pounds; about one hundred and twenty gallons of water yield sixty pounds of salt. The large tract of land reserved is devoted solely to the purpose of making salt, no part of it being leased for tillage; the object of this regulation is to preserve a supply of timber for fuel. Beds of stone-coal have recently been discovered near the furnaces, but they have not yet been brought into use. The constitution of this state, while it prohibited slavery, allowed the salt makers to hire slaves within the Saline boundary, until the expiration of the year 1825. While this privilege, which was suggested by the scarcity of labourers in a new country, continued to exist, the labour of salt making was performed by negroes, hired from the people of Kentucky and Tennessee. A temporary suspension of operations has been caused by the change from the old to the new order of things. What will be the ultimate effect of the new system is bare matter of conjecture; the better opinion seems to be that the change will be beneficial.

LETTER XV.

NATIONAL CHARACTER.

DEAR N.

IF in the little circle of my intellectual pleasures, there is one which affords me more
enjoyment than any other, it consists in tracing
the varieties of character which exist in the
different branches of our great national family.
It is interesting to observe, how soon every
new country—nay, even every little colony,
adopts some trait of habit or manners peculiar
to itself. These may be ascribed to local circumstances—climate, soil, and situation, all
contribute to produce them. The keen blast
that invigorates the frame, or the sultry beam
that relaxes the system, induces a correspondent effect upon the mind; abundance
leads to luxury; while the inhabitant of a

niggard soil, must be frugal and industrious. But there are a thousand other causes which produce particular customs in particular places; and this diversity, which to me is highly entertaining, affords an ample fund of vexation to the fastidious, and makes room for innumerable sarcasms from those travellers who delight in ridiculing every thing which does not exactly accord with their own habits or notions of propriety. One of Shakspeare's contemporaries, in speaking of him, says, " Ben Jonson and he did gather humours of men dayly, wherever they came." We have seen how our great dramatist profited by this employment ; but our modern travellers seem rather disposed to get rid of their own *humours,* than to collect those of other people. But ridicule is not the test of truth ; and it might puzzle those gentlemen to give a good reason why their own customs are intrinsically better than those which amuse them abroad : you may smile at the rings in an Indian lady's nose ; but why should they not be as graceful as those in the American lady's ears ?

The American colonies were peopled from

Great Britain, and the western states derive
their inhabitants, chiefly, from New England and
Virginia. Yet when the American looks back
at his British ancestor, he discovers few traits of
similarity; and the back-woodsman is almost
as far removed from his eastern progenitor.
In the great matters of religion and law, all
of us in the United States are the same—as the
children of one family, when they separate in
the world, still preserve the impress of those
principles which they imbibed from a common
source; but, in all matters of taste and fancy,
customs and exterior deportment, we find a
variance. Those who live under the same
government, participate in the same laws, and
profess the same religion—whose representa-
tives mingle in council, whose warriors rally
under the same banner, who celebrate the
same victories, and mourn for the same disas-
ters—must have many feelings and sentiments
in common, though they may differ in their
modes of evincing them. Thus he who would
attempt to pourtray the American character,
must draw, not a single portrait, but a family-
piece, containing several heads. In each of

these would be discovered some strong lines
common to all : the same active, enterprising,
and independent spirit ; the same daring soul,
and inventive genius; and that aptitude or
capacity to take advantage of every change,
and subsist and flourish in every soil and situation. But each would have a shade or cast
of expression peculiar to itself ; and, at the first
glance, there would be seen no more resem-
blance between the Boston merchant, the
Virginia planter, and the hunter of the west,
than if they had sprung from different
sources. Observe them more closely, however,
or rouse their energies into action, and you will
still find, in each section of our country, the
same American spirit, which glowed in the
breasts of Putnam, of Marion, and of Wayne.
Show me a strong line in the south, and I will
point out to you a kindred feature in the north ;
produce a *Jackson* from the west, and I will bring
you a *Perry* from the east. In private life,
the amiable, unassuming Rhode Islander might
present a striking contrast to the fiery Tennes-
sean : but the soul of the hero burned with not
less ardour on Lake Erie —the light of the vic-

tory was not less brilliant than that which
blazed at New Orleans.

Thence it is that foreigners err when they
give a character to our whole population from
observations made in a single sea-port ; or when
they allow us no national character at all, because they discover traits in different places
which seem to be the very antipodes of each
other. In this latter sapient hypothesis, they
evince, together with a good deal of ignorance,
not a little of that insolence which distinguishes
our foreign detractors. There is no people in
the world whose national character is better
defined or more strongly marked than our
own. If the European theory on this subject
be correct, is it not a little strange, that our
Yankee tars, whether on board of a frigate or
a privateer, should always *happen* to play the
same game, when they come athwart an Englishman ? Is it not a little singular, that
Brown in the North, and Jackson in the South,
who I suspect never saw each other in their
lives, should always *happen* to handle Lord
Wellington's veterans exactly after the same
fashion ? Accidents *will* happen in the best of

families; but when an accident occurs in the same family repeatedly, we are apt to suspect that it runs in the blood.

In the different states there is certainly a great disparity in the manners of the people. In New England the soil is not rich, and the population is dense. The mass of the people are, of course, laborious, close, and frugal. The colonists were men of pure manners and religious habits. In all their municipal regulations, the suppression of vice and immorality, or rather the *exclusion* of them, for they had none to suppress, formed a leading principle. Persons of this character, would probably be inclined to lead domestic lives, and be satisfied with cheap and innocent amusements. Thus every man, happy in the society of his family and his neighbours, preferred the little circle in which he found content and cheerfulness, to all the world besides. Not sufficiently wealthy to be seduced by the Syren song of pleasure, nor so poor as to become debased by want, he neither spurned nor courted the stranger that approached his door. He was not unwilling to perform an act of charity or kindness, nor ashamed to offer what his humble board afforded; but he wished to know something of the character of the person whom he received into his friendship, whose vices might injure him in his substance, or whose licentiousness might contaminate the morals of his children. The man whose *home* is thus the sphere of his usefulness and the scene of his enjoyments, must feel deeply interested in every object around him; the conduct of his neighbours, the morals of his servants, and the minds of his children, concern him too nearly to be neglected. Thus he is apt to become not only an industrious and virtuous citizen himself, but a watchful observer of the conduct of others. Such were the manners of the primitive settlers in New England, and such they remain in many parts of it to this day. But their local situation was not such as to allow them to retain their rural character in its pristine chastity. In repelling the hostile incursions which threatened to destroy their infant settlements, they acquired confidence in their courage, and many of their youth imbibed a military spirit, which rendered their former avocations insipid. The situation of their country, bounded by an extensive sea-coast, indented with noble harbours, presented commercial advantages too inviting to be neglected; and the enterprising temper of the people soon rendered them as conspicuous among the hardy sons of the ocean as they had been exemplary in more peaceful scenes. The commercial spirit, thus engrafted upon the " steady habits" of these people, has given them a cast of character peculiar to themselves. Hardy and independent; ingenious in devising, and indefatigable in executing any plan of which the end is gain; pursuing their designs with ardour and enthusiasm, yet adhering to them constantly, conducting them prudently, and concealing them artfully, if necessary, there is no people so versatile in their genius, and none so universally successful in their undertakings.

In their own country, there is no people more domestic : yet, strange to tell, they are to be found scattered in the four corners of the earth, every where adopting the manners of those around them, and flourishing, even in the midst of ruin; so that it has become proverbial, that a Yankee

R

may live where another man would starve. The poorest people in that country receive the first rudiments of education ; and from this source, perhaps, they derive a trait which is the greatest blemish in their character. " A little learning" has been said to be " a dangerous thing ;" and from that source, I am inclined to believe, we derive that species of *finesse*, commonly called *Yankee tricks*. The New Englanders are remarkable for their shrewdness, or what the Irish call " mother wit ;" and when such a man happens to have a bad heart, or loose principles, "a little learning" is really a dangerous accession of strength. He that has the *ability* to deceive, without the moral principle to control the evil propensities of human nature, or without sufficient weight of character to enlist *pride* as an auxiliary, must be exposed to temptations too strong for flesh and blood to resist. A man of colder temperament, or less ingenuity, would neither have the inclination to attempt, the wit to devise, nor the address to execute, that which a Yankee undertakes with the utmost *sang froid*. They are indeed, like Caleb Quotem, " up to

every thing"—as the poet says. This, at first
sight, appears to be a stigma on the character
of our eastern brethren; but when we recollect
that it is confined to a portion of the population, and that portion among the lower classes,
it would seem but fair to attribute it to the
frailty of human nature, rather than to the
want of national virtue.

In Virginia we find different manners. The
white population is less dense, and the country
less commercial. Most of the gentlemen are
born gentlemen; they are wealthy, and receive
liberal educations ; from their cradles they
despise money, because they are not in the
habit of seeing those with whom they associate
actively engaged in the pursuit of it. The
slaves perform all the labour, leaving their
masters at liberty to cultivate their minds and
enjoy the society of their friends. The most
numerous class is composed of the *planters,*
and these are accomplished gentlemen, residing
on their own estates, fond of pleasure, and
princes in hospitality. Kentucky having been
settled by Virginians, the manners of the people
are nearly the same, except that the latter, living

in a more fertile country, are perhaps, more profuse in their generosity.

Now these two sections of our country have the same American character. The people in both are high minded, spirited lovers of liberty, tenacious of their honour, and quick in their resentments; they equally loathe every thing in the shape of oppression, encroachment, or dictation; they claim the same right of instructing their officers, and exercise the same power of dismissing them on the slightest provocation. But then these qualities, which are common to our country, display themselves differently in different situations; they are compressed or expanded by circumstances. In one section the people are in the habit of curbing their passions, and refraining from those pleasures which are inconvenient or expensive; in the other, they are more accustomed to indulge the propensities of their nature. They both have those generous feelings, which must always form a part of the character of a free, brave, and enlightened people; but one has wealth and leisure to yield full play to all the impulses of the heart, which the other must restrain.

In New England, and still more in the middle states, the want of servants is a great drawback upon social intercourse. Where the lady of the house for instance, must go into her kitchen to superintend the preparation of a meal, or to dress herself, and after hastily arranging her dress, return with a blowzed face to do the honours of her table, too much fatigued to enjoy its pleasures, the visit of a stranger must afford less pleasure than where such inconveniences do not occur. The New Englander, therefore, will be *politely civil* from a sense of *duty*, where the Virginian is *profusely hospitable* from generous feelings, and because he can enjoy the pleasures of society without its inconveniences.

But take the Virginian from his plantation, or the Yankee from his boat and harpoon, or from his snug cottage, his stone fences, his " neatly white-washed walls," his blooming garden and his tasteful grounds, and place him in a wilderness, with an axe in his hand or a rifle on his shoulder, and he soon becomes a different man ; his *national character* will burst the chains of local habit. He does not, like the European in the same situation, languish for want of luxuries which he cannot procure, or groan under hardships from which he cannot fly. His ingenuity supplies him with new sources of livelihood, his courage with new vigour; his hardy frame and versatile spirit easily accommodate themselves to new employments : and though he has still the same heart, the same feelings, and the same principles, he is quite another person in his manners and mode of living.

In some of the middle states the national character is not so well defined, as there is a greater mixture of people. In the interior of Pennsylvania, there are large settlements of Irish and Dutch, or their immediate descendants, who have not yet inhaled our atmosphere long enough to acquire the peculiar characteristics of Americans ; but there is no doubt that they, and even the English emigrants, when they have vegetated for a few generations in our happy country, will become estimable citizens.

This subject might be pursued with advantage, but having thrown out the hints, I leave you to speculate upon them. My object is only to gather the raw materials which may be woven by more skilful hands; you must judge *ex pede Herculem*, of the whole from a part. Any person who is acquainted with the spirit of our constitution and laws, and the general description of our country, will be able to supply my defects from his own imagination, and to deduce a variety of inferences from the propositions which I have stated. That we have a national character cannot be denied; that that character is an estimable one, will I think not be doubted; and that a part of it consists in loving our homes, and cherishing our friends, you will believe on the word of

Your affectionate, &c.

LETTER XVI.

BACKWOODSMEN.

It is but a few years since the immense tract of country watered by the Ohio and Mississippi, began to attract the attention of our countrymen. The French had long before formed settlements on the Mississippi and the Wabash, and on the northern lakes; but these insulated situations were so much exposed to Indian hostility, and the dispositions of the inhabitants were so uncongenial with the habits of our people, that they were at first visited only by a few enterprising traders. As the country became better known, report spoke goldenly of its fertility, and a casual reference to the map was sufficient to show the great commercial advantages to be derived from the numerous and valuable streams which intersect it in every direction; but there

were many obstacles to its settlement. From
a period shortly after the revolution to the time
of the embargo in 1807, there was no reason
to induce any class of citizens in the United
States to emigrate; all were fully and profitably
employed at home. The sanguinary wars which
spread desolation thoughout the European con-
tinent, not only opened markets for all our
surplus produce, but made us the carriers of
other nations. Never did American enterprise
shine more conspicuously than in the improvement of these advantages: the art of ship-
building was brought to a perfection unknown in
any other country; our flag floated in every part
of the world; there was no adventure, however
novel or hazardous, which our merchants did
not attempt; and our sailors displayed on every
occasion the skill and boldness which has since
made them conspicuous in the annals of naval
warfare. Happily too, those enterprises were
generally successful. The consequence was,
that every man engaged in commercial pursuits
found sufficient employment for his capital,
while the labouring classes received high wages,
and the farmer had always a ready market and

an ample price for his produce. This flourishing state of commerce and agriculture diffused life and spirit into every rank and department of society. There was scarcely such a thing known as a man labouring merely to *support his family ;* no one was satisfied unless he was growing rich, and few were disappointed except by their own improvidence. It would be useless to point out the great statesmen and lawyers who have attained their present eminence from an obscure origin, or the wealthy merchants, farmers, and mechanics, who, from the most abject poverty, have risen to opulence. Our country is full of such examples, and they stand as monuments of those happy days when industry was not only a sure but a rapid guide to wealth.

Under such circumstances, few persons were disposed to emigrate to a new country; and although some were tempted by the great prospects of gain which the fertile regions in the west were said to offer, many were discouraged by the unsettled state of the country, its reputed unhealthiness, and the vicinity of the Indian tribes.

To Europeans this part of America offered no attractions : it was too remote, too insulated, too barbarous, and too entirely uncongenial with all their habits, tastes, and feelings.

The first settlers of this country, therefore, were men whose object was not gain, but who appeared to have been allured by the very difficulties which discouraged others. They were hardy, enterprising men, fond of chance, and familiar with fatigue, who seem to have thought with Fitz James—

> " If a path be dangerous known,
> The danger's self is lure alone."

Colonel Boon, the chief of these, and the first white inhabitant of Kentucky, died lately. His name deserves to be recorded, not only on account of his dauntless courage and eccentric habits, but because his life and achievements present a glowing picture of the sufferings of those who subdued the western forests ; he stands forward, too, as a prominent individual of a class peculiar to the United States. The American who takes a retrospective view of the early history of his country, must regard with admiration the sturdy woodsman, who, as the pioneer of civilization, first laid the axe to the tree, and made smooth the road for others ; but he will find him an isolated being, professing tastes and habits of his own, and voluntarily supporting incredible hardships, peril, and privation, without the usual incentives or the ordinary rewards of courage.

In the year 1769, Daniel Boon, a respectable farmer of North Carolina, was led by a restless, migratory spirit into the forests of Kentucky' then an extensive wilderness, inhabited by numberless savage tribes, and as yet unexplored by civilized man. Passing the Alleghany Ridge, whose hideous precipices alone might have repelled a less determined band—guided only by the stars—depending on game for subsistence, and on their own vigilance and prowess for protection—Boon, with five adventurous companions, plunged into *the boundless contiguity of shade*, and boldly cut the tie which bound them to society. The mariner, when he looks abroad upon the vast interminable waste, may feel a depressing, yet awful and sublime sense of danger and solitude ; but he has the consolation of knowing that if the solitude of the ocean be hopeless, its dangers are few and easily surmounted : they exist rather in idea than in reality. Boon and his companions could have had no such animating reflections. In a country called the " Bloody Ground," from the extirminating character of its conflicts ;—among savage tribes, continually at war with each other, and agreeing in nothing but their deadly enmity to the whites—cut off from society— with scanty means of defence, and no hope of retreat,—we scarcely know whether to extol the courage, or censure the rashness of this gallant little party. They continued in Kentucky until the year 1775, leading a wandering life, employed chiefly in exploring the country, and frequently engaged in conflicts with the Indians. In 1775, Boon erected a fort at a *salt lick*, on the Kentucky River, where the town of Boonsborough now stands, which was called Fort Boonsborough, and to which he removed his family in the same year. " My wife and daughters," says he, in his journal, " were the first white women that ever stood on the banks of the Kentucky River." Here he was joined by five families from North Carolina, and forty men from Powell's Valley. During the years 1775-6-7, Fort Boonsborough was frequently attacked by the Indians, and several severe engagements took place, in which the savages were always repulsed.

Boon's settlement began now to exhibit something like a permanent residence of civilized men. The forest was levelled around the fort, fields were enclosed and cultivated, and rustic labours were mingled with the business of war, and the sports of the chase. Their numbers were now sufficient, in general, to prevent surprise; and in case of danger, the fortress offered a secure retreat. Nevertheless, in January 1778, while Boon was engaged with a party of twenty-seven men in making salt at the *Blue Lick*, they were surprised and taken by a large body of Indians, who were on their way to attack the fort, and conveyed to Chilicothe, on the Little Miami, then a considerable Indian town. In the month of March following, Boon was carried with ten of his men to Detroit, where the party was well treated by the British Governor, Hamilton, as indeed they had hitherto been by the Indians, agreeably to a stipulation made at the time of their capture. The gallant bearing of Boon, and his skill in hunting, had by this time, endeared him to the Indians, so that although the British officers offered a hundred pounds sterling for him, with the intention of setting him at liberty, they would not sell him, nor would they allow him to remain a prisoner with his companions at Detroit, but took him back with them to Chilicothe. " Here," says his journal, " I was adopted into the family of a chief as a son, which is their custom, and permitted to hunt and spend my time as I pleased. In June following they took me to Sciota Salt Springs, where we continued making salt for ten days. On our return to Old Chilicothe, I was alarmed to see four hundred and fifty Indians, the choicest of their warriors, painted and armed in a fearful manner, and ready as I found to march against Boonsborough. I now determined to make my escape on the first opportunity; there was no time to be lost. On the 16th, before sun-rise, I got off in the most secret manner, and on the 20th, arrived at Boonsborough, a distance of one hundred and sixty miles, while travelling which I had but one meal. I found our fort in a state; all hands were engaged earnestly in repairing and fortifying it in the best manner possible for the impending blow of the enemy, whose arrival was expected daily. Some time previous to my capture, a re-inforcement of forty-five men arrived from North Carolina, and Colonel Brown with one hundred men from Virginia; and notwithstanding we had lost some in killed and others wounded, we considered ourselves pretty strong, and determined to brave all dangers. We were in waiting for the enemy, when we got information that they had postponed their march for two weeks, in consequence of my escape from them; in the meantime, we had several skirmishes with small parties of the Indians. On the 8th of August, however, the ferocious Indian army arrived, four hundred and forty-four in number, under the command of Captain Duquesne, eleven other Frenchmen, and some of their own chiefs, and marched up within view of the fort with British and French colours flying. They halted, and despatched a summons to me, in His Britannic

Majesty s name to surrender the fort ; to this I
returned for answer that I wanted two days to
consider of it, which was granted.

"It was now a critical time with us. We
were a small number in the garrison ; a powerful, cruel, and savage army lay before our
stockaded fort, whose appearance proclaimed
inevitable death. We immediately began to
collect what number of our horses and cattle
we could, and bring them through the posterns
into the fort. On the evening of the 9th, I
returned answer, that we were determined to
defend our fort while a man was living.
'Now,' said I to their commanding-officer,
who stood attentively hearing my sentiments,
' we laugh at all your formidable preparations,
but thank you for giving us notice and time
to prepare ; your efforts will not prevail ;
our gates shall even deny you admittance.'
Whether this answer affected their courage or
not, I cannot tell, but contrary to our expectations, they formed a scheme to deceive us,
declaring it was their orders from Governor
Hamilton to take us captives ; but if nine of us
would come out and treat with them, they

s

would withdraw their forces and return home
peaceably. The sound of this proposition was
grateful to our ears, and we agreed to the pro-
posal.

" We held the treaty within sixty yards of
the garrison, fearing that treachery was at the
bottom of this manœuvre; the articles were
formally agreed to and signed, and the Indians
told us it was customary with them on such
occasions, for *two Indians* to shake hands with
every white man in the treaty, as an evidence
of entire friendship. We agreed to this also,
but were soon convinced they were determined
to take us prisoners. They immediately grappled with us; and, although surrounded by
hundreds of savages, we extricated ourselves
from them, and got into the garrison all safe,
one man excepted, who was wounded. A furious
attack was now made on us from all sides, and
a constant heavy fire continued between us day
and night for nine days, during which they
attempted to undermine our fort. We began a
countermine, which they discovered, and, in consequence, they quitted this project. They now
began to be convinced that neither their stra-

tagems nor superior force was likely to overcome us, and on the 20th of August, they
raised the siege and departed."

You must excuse this long extract, which I
think highly interesting from the evidence it
affords of the heroic character of our woodsmen.
Boon was the chief of these, the very prince
of hunters. If many of the heroes of Greece and
Rome, derived immortal fame from a single act
of heroism, how much more does Boon deserve
it, whose whole life presents a series of adventures of the same character as those which I
have related? Nor did he suffer and conquer
alone; his wife accompanied him to the wilderness, and shared his dangers; during his
captivity, under a belief that he had fallen a
sacrifice to the ferocity of the savage foe, she
returned with her family to her father's house
in North Carolina, braving the toil and perils
of a journey, through a wilderness of immeasur-
able extent and gloom. She remained there till
after the siege, when Boon escorted her back to
Boonsborough.

Another incident which occurred here is not
only deeply interesting in itself, but is highly

illustrative of the sufferings of the first settlers. Among the adventurers whom Boon described as having re-inforced his little colony, was a young gentleman named Smith, who had been a major in the militia of Virginia, and possessed a full share of the gallantry and noble spirit of his native state. In the absence of Boon, he was chosen, on account of his military rank and talents, to command the rude citadel, which contained all the wealth of this patriarchal band—their wives, their children, and their herds. It held also an object particularly dear to this young soldier—a lady, the daughter of one of the settlers, to whom he had pledged his affections. It came to pass, upon a certain day, when the siege was over, tranquillity restored, and the employments of husbandry resumed, that this young lady with a female companion strolled out, as young ladies in love are very apt to do, along the banks of the Kentucky River. Having rambled about for some time, they espied a canoe lying by the shore, and in a frolic stepped into it, with the determination of visiting a neighbour on the opposite bank. It seems that they were not so well skilled in navigation as the *Lady of the Lake*, who " paddled her own canoe" very dexterously ;—for instead of gliding to the point of destination, they were whirled about by the stream, and at length thrown on a sand-bar, from which they were obliged to wade to the shore. Full of the mirth excited by their wild adventure, they hastily arranged their dresses, and were proceeding to climb the banks when three Indians, rushing from a neighbouring covert, seized the fair wanderers, and forced them away. Their savage captors, evincing no sympathy for their distress, nor allowing them time for rest or reflection, hurried them along during the whole day by rugged and thorny paths. Their shoes were worn off by the rocks, their clothes torn, and their feet and limbs lacerated, and stained with blood. To heighten their misery, one of the savages began to make love to Miss ——, (the *intended* of Major S.), and while goading her along with a pointed stick, promised, in recompense for her sufferings, to make her *his squaw*. This at once roused all the energies of her mind, and called its powers into action. In the hope that her friends would soon pursue them, she broke the twigs as she passed along, and delayed the party as much as possible by tardy and blundering steps. But why dwell on the heartless and unmanly cruelty of these savages? The day and the night passed, and another day of agony had nearly rolled over the heads of these afflicted females, when their conductors halted to cook a wild repast of buffalo meat.

The ladies were soon missed from the garrison. The natural courage and sagacity of Smith, now heightened by love, gave him the wings of the wind and the fierceness of the tiger. The light traces of female feet led him to the place of embarkation,—the canoe was traced to the opposite shore—the deep print of the moccasin in the sand told the rest ; and the agonized Smith, accompanied by a few of his best woodsmen, pursued "the spoil-encumbered foe." The track, once discovered, they kept it with that unerring sagacity so peculiar to our hunters. The bended grass, the disentangled briars, and the compressed shrub, afforded the only, but to them the certain, indications of the route of the enemy. When they had sufficiently

ascertained the general course of the retreat of
the Indians, Smith quitted the trace, assuring
his companions that they would fall in with them
at the pass of a certain stream ahead, for which
he now struck a direct course, thus gaining on
the foe, who had taken the most difficult paths.
Arrived at the stream, they traced its course
until they discovered the water newly thrown
upon the rocks. Smith, leaving his party, now
crept forward upon his hands and feet, until he
discovered one of the savages seated by a fire,
and with a deliberate aim shot him through the
heart. The women rushed towards their
deliverer, and recognizing Smith, clung to him
in the transports of newly awakened joy and
gratitude, while a second Indian sprang towards
him with his tomahawk. Smith disengaging
himself from the ladies, aimed a blow at his
antagonist with his rifle, which the savage
avoided by springing aside, but at the same
moment the latter received a mortal wound
from another hand. The other and only
remaining Indian fell in attempting to escape.
Smith, with his interesting charge, returned in

triumph to the fort, where his gallantry, no doubt, was repaid by the sweetest of all rewards.

This romantic little story, which is all true, I have taken from the "Western Review," published at Lexington, Kentucky; but in abridging it, I have not been able to retain the beauties which embellished the original recital. From the initial affixed to it in that work, I presume that it is from the pen of a gentleman who has enriched the literature of the west with much curious and authentic information on the subject of Indian antiquities.

LETTER XVII.

THE HARPES.

MANY years ago, two men, named Harpe, appeared in Kentucky, spreading death and terror wherever they went. Little else was known of them but that they passed for brothers, and came from the borders of Virginia. They had three women with them, who were treated as their wives, and several children, with whom they traversed the mountainous and thinly settled parts of Virginia into Kentucky, marking their course with blood. Their history is wonderful, as well from the number and variety, as the incredible atrocity of their adventures; and as it has never yet appeared in print, I shall compress within this letter a few of its most prominent facts.

In the autumn of the year 1799, a young gentleman, named Langford, of a respectable family in Mecklenburgh county, Virginia, set out from this state for Kentucky, with the intention of passing through the *Wilderness*, as it was then called, by the route generally known as *Boon's Trace*. On reaching the vicinity of the wilderness, a mountainous and uninhabited tract, which at that time separated the settled parts of Kentucky from those of Virginia, he stopped to breakfast at a public house near Big Rock-castle River. Travellers of this description—any other indeed than hardy woodsmen—were unwilling to pass singly through this lonely region ; and they generally waited on its confines for others, and travelled through in parties. Mr. Langford, either not dreading danger, or not choosing to delay, determined to proceed alone. While breakfast was preparing, the Harpes and their women came up. Their appearance denoted poverty, with but little regard to cleanliness ; two very indifferent horses, with some bags swung across them, and a rifle gun or two, composed nearly their whole equipage. Squalid and miserable, they seemed objects of pity, rather than of fear, and their ferocious glances were attributed more to hunger than to guilty passion. They were entire strangers in that neighbourhood, and, like Mr. Langford, were about to cross the Wilderness. When breakfast was served up, the landlord, as was customary at such places, in those times, invited all the persons who were assembled in the common, perhaps the only room of his little inn, to sit down; but the Harpes declined, alleging their want of money as the reason. Langford, who was of a lively, generous disposition, on hearing this invited them to partake of the meal at his expense; they accepted the invitation, and eat voraciously. When they had thus refreshed themselves, and were about to renew their journey Mr. Langford called for the bill, and in the act of discharging it imprudently displayed a handful of silver. They then set out together.

A few days after, some men who were conducting a drove of cattle to Virginia, by the same road which had been travelled by Mr.

Langford and the Harpes, had arrived within a few miles of Big Rock-castle River, when their cattle took fright, and, quitting the road, rushed down a hill into the woods. In collecting them, the drovers discovered the dead body of a man concealed behind a log, and covered with brush and leaves. It was now evident that the cattle had been alarmed by the smell of blood in the road, and as the body exhibited marks of violence, it was at once suspected that a murder had been perpetrated but recently. The corpse was taken to the same house where the Harpes had breakfasted, and recognised to be that of Mr. Langford, whose name was marked upon several parts of his dress. Suspicion fell upon the Harpes, who were pursued and apprehended near the *Crab Orchard*. They were taken to Stanford, the seat of justice for Lincoln county, where they were examined and committed by an inquiring court, sent to Danville for safe keeping, and probably for trial, as the system of *district* courts was then in operation in Kentucky. Previous to the time of trial, they made their escape, and proceeded to Henderson county, which at that time was just beginning to be settled.

Here they soon acquired a dreadful celebrity. Neither avarice, want, nor any of the usual inducements to the commission of crime, seemed to govern their conduct. A savage thirst for blood—a deep rooted malignity against human nature, could alone be discovered in their actions. They murdered every defenceless being who fell in their way without distinction of age, sex, or colour. In the night they stole secretly to the cabin, slaughtered its inhabitants, and burned their dwelling—while the farmer who left his house by day, returned to witness the dying agonies of his wife and children, and the conflagration of his possessions. Plunder was not their object : travellers they robbed and murdered, but from the inhabitants they took only what would have been freely given to them, and no more than was immediately necessary to supply the wants of nature ; they destroyed without having suffered injury, and without the prospect of gain. A negro boy, riding to a mill, with a bag of corn, was seized by them, and his brains dashed out against a tree ; but the horse which he rode and the grain were left unmolested. Females, children, and servants, no longer dared to stir abroad ; unarmed men feared to encounter a Harpe ; and the solitary hunter, as he trod the forest, looked around him with a watchful eye, and when he saw a stranger, picked his flint and stood on the defensive.

It seems incredible that such atrocities could have been often repeated in a country famed for the hardihood and gallantry of its people ; in Kentucky, the cradle of courage, and the nurse of warriors. But that part of Kentucky which was the scene of these barbarities was then almost a wilderness, and the vigilance of the Harpes for a time ensured impunity. The spoils of their dreadful warfare furnished them with the means of violence and of escape. Mounted on fine horses, they plunged into the forest, eluded pursuit by frequently changing their course, and appeared, unexpectedly, to perpetrate new enormities, at points distant from those where they were supposed to lurk. On these occasions, they often left their wives and children behind them ; and it is a fact, honourable to the community, that vengeance for these bloody deeds, was not wreaked on the helpless, but in some degree guilty, companions of the perpetrators. Justice, however, was not long delayed.

A frontier is often the retreat of loose individuals, who, if not familiar with crime, have very blunt perceptions of virtue. The genuine woodsman, the real pioneer, are independent, brave, and upright; but as the jackal pursues the lion to devour his leavings, the footsteps of the sturdy hunter are closely pursued by miscreants destitute of his noble qualities. These are the poorest and the idlest of the human race—averse to labour, and impatient of the restraints of law and the courtesies of civilized society. Without the ardour, the activity, the love of sport, and patience of fatigue, which distinguish the bold backwoodsman, these are doomed to the forest by sheer laziness, and hunt for a bare subsistence ; they are the " cankers of a calm world and a long peace," the helpless *nobodies,* who, in a country where none starve and few beg, sleep until hunger pinches,

then stroll into the woods for a meal, and return
to their slumber.   Frequently they are as harm-
less as the wart upon a man's nose, and as unsightly; but they are sometimes mere wax in
the hands of the designing, and become the
accessories of that guilt which they have not
the courage or the industry to perpetrate.
With such men the Harpes are supposed to
have sometimes lurked.   None are known to
have participated in their deeds of blood, nor
suspected of sharing their counsels; but they
sometimes crept to the miserable cabins of
those who feared or were not inclined to betray
them.

Two travellers came one night to the house
of a man named Stegal, and, for want of better
lodgings, claimed under his little roof that
hospitality which in a new country is found at
every habitation.   Shortly after, the Harpes
arrived.   It was not, it seems, their first visit ;
for Mrs. Stegal had received instructions from
them, which she dared not disobey, never to
address them by their real names in the presence of third persons.   On this occasion they
contrived to inform her that they intended to

personate *methodist preachers*, and ordered her
to arrange matters so that one of them should
sleep with each of the strangers, whom they
intended to murder. Stegal was absent, and
the woman was obliged to obey. The strangers
were completely deceived as to the character
of the newly arrived guests; and when it was
announced that the house contained but two
beds, they cheerfully assented to the proposed
arrangement: one crept into a bed on the
lower floor with one ruffian, while the other
retired to the loft with another. Both the
strangers became their victims; but these
bloody ruffians, who seemed neither to feel
shame, nor dread punishment, determined to
leave behind them no evidence of their crime,
and consummated the foul tragedy by murdering
their hostess and setting fire to the dwelling.

From this scene of arson, robbery, and murder, the perpetrators fled precipitately, favoured
by a heavy fall of rain, which, as they believed,
effaced their footsteps. They did not cease
their flight until late the ensuing day, when
they halted at a spot which they supposed to
be far from any human habitation. Here they

T

kindled a fire, and were drying their clothes, when an emigrant, who had pitched his tent hard by, strolled towards their camp. He was in search of his horses, which had strayed, and civilly asked if they had seen them. This unsuspecting woodsman they slew, and continued their retreat.

In the meanwhile, the outrages of these murderers had not escaped notice, nor were they tamely submitted to. The Governor of Kentucky had offered a reward for their heads, and parties of volunteers had pursued them; they had been so fortunate as to escape punishment by their cunning, but had not the prudence to desist, or to fly the country.

A man, named Leiper, in revenge for the murder of Mrs. Stegal, raised a party, pursued, and discovered the assassins, on the day succeeding that atrocious deed. They came so suddenly upon the Harpes that they had only time to fly in different directions. Accident aided the pursuers. One of the Harpes was a large, and the other a small man; the first usually rode a strong, powerful horse, the other a fleet, but much smaller animal, and in the hurry of flight they had exchanged horses. The chase was long and hot: the smaller Harpe escaped unnoticed; but the other, who was kept in view, spurred on the noble animal which he rode, and which, already jaded, began to fail at the end of five or six miles. Still the miscreant pressed forward; for, although none of his pursuers were near but Leiper, who had outridden his companions, he was not willing to risk a combat with a man as strong and perhaps bolder than himself, who was animated with a noble spirit of indignation against a shocking and unmanly outrage. Leiper was mounted upon a horse of celebrated powers, which he had borrowed from a neighbour for this occasion. At the beginning of the chase, he had pressed his charger to the height of his speed, carefully keeping on the track of Harpe, of whom he sometimes caught a glimpse as he ascended the hills, and again lost sight in the valleys and the brush. But as he gained on the foe, and became sure of his victim, he slackened his pace, cocked his rifle, and deliberately pursued, sometimes calling upon the outlaw to surrender. At length, in leaping a ravine, Harpe's horse sprained a limb, and Leiper overtook him. Both were armed with rifles. Leiper fired, and wounded Harpe through the body ; the latter, turning in his seat, levelled his piece, which missed fire, and he dashed it to the ground, swearing it was the first time it had ever deceived him. He then drew a tomahawk, and waited the approach of Leiper, who, nothing daunted, unsheathed his long hunting knife and rushed upon his desperate foe, grappled with him, hurled him to the ground, and wrested his only remaining weapon from his grasp. The prostrate wretch—exhausted with the loss of blood, conquered, but unsubdued in spirit—now lay passive at the feet of his adversary. Expecting every moment the arrival of the rest of his pursuers, he inquired if Stegal was of the party, and being answered in the affirmative, he exclaimed, " then I am a dead man."

"That would make no difference," replied Leiper, calmly ; " you must die at any rate. I do not wish to kill you myself, but if nobody else will do it, I must." Leiper was a humane man, easy, slow-spoken, and not quickly excited, but a thorough soldier when roused. Without insulting the expiring criminal, he questioned him as to the motives of his late atrocities. The murderer attempted not to palliate or deny them, and confessed that he had been actuated by no inducement but a settled hatred of his species, whom he had sworn to destroy without distinction, in retaliation for some fancied injury. He expressed no regret for any of his bloody deeds, except that which he confessed he had perpetrated upon *one of his own children.* " It cried," said he, " and I killed it: I had always told the women, I would have no crying about me." He acknowledged that he had amassed large sums of money, and described the places of concealment; but as none was ever discovered, it is presumed he did not declare the truth. Leiper had fired several times at Harpe during the chase, and wounded him; and when the latter was asked why, when he found Leiper pursuing him alone, he did not dismount and *take to a tree,* from behind which he could inevitably have shot him as he approached, he replied that he had supposed there was not a horse in the country equal to the one which he rode, and that he was confident of making his escape. He thought also that the pursuit would be less eager, so long as he abstained from shedding the blood of any of his pursuers. On the arrival of the rest of the party, the wretch was dispatched, and he died as he had lived, in remorseless guilt. It is said, however, that he was about to make some disclosure, and had commenced in a tone of more sincerity than he had before evinced, when Stegal advanced and severed his head from his body. This bloody trophy they carried to the nearest magistrate, a Mr. Newman, before whom it was proved to be the head of Micajah Harpe; they then placed it in the fork of a tree, where it long remained a revolting object of horror. The spot which is near the Highland Lick, in Union (then Henderson) County, is still called *Harpe's Head*, and a public road which passes it, is called the Harpe's Head Road.

The other Harpe made his way to the neighbourhood of Natchez, where he joined a gang of robbers, headed by a man named Meason, whose villanies were so notorious that a reward was offered for his head. At that period, vast regions along the shores of the Ohio and

Mississippi were still unsettled, through which boats navigating those rivers must necessarily pass; and the traders who, after selling their cargoes at New Orleans, attempted to return by land, had to cross immense wildernesses, totally destitute of inhabitants. Meason, who was a man rather above the ordinary stamp, infested these deserts, seldom committing murder, but robbing all who fell in his way. Sometimes he plundered the descending boats; but more frequently he allowed these to pass, preferring to rob their owners of their money as they returned, pleasantly observing, that "those people were taking produce to market for him." Harpe took an opportunity, when the rest of his companions were absent, to slay Meason, and putting his head in a bag, carried it to Natchez, and claimed the reward. The claim was admitted; the head of Meason was recognized; but so also was the face of Harpe, who was arrested, condemned, and executed.

In collecting oral testimony of events long past, a considerable variety will often be found in the statements of the persons conversant with the circumstances. In this case, I have

found none, except as to the fact of the two
Harpes having exchanged horses. A day or two
before the fatal catastrophe which ended their
career in Kentucky, they had murdered a
gentleman named Love, and had taken his
horse, a remarkably fine animal, which big
Harpe undoubtedly rode when he was overtaken. It is said that Little Harpe escaped on
foot, and not on his brother's horse. Many of
these facts were disclosed by the latter, while
under sentence of death.

After Harpe's death the women came in
and claimed protection. Two of them were the
wives of the larger Harpe, the other one of
his brother. The latter was a decent female, of
delicate, prepossessing appearance, who stated
that she had married her husband without any
knowledge of his real character, shortly before
they set out for the west ; that she was so much
shocked at the first murder which they committed, that she attempted to escape from them,
but was prevented, and that she had since made
similar attempts. She immediately wrote to
her father in Virginia, who came for her, and
took her home. The other women were in no

way remarkable. They remained in Muhlen-burgh county.

These horrid events will sound like fiction to your ears, when told as having happened in any part of the United States, so foreign are they from the generosity of the American character, the happy security of our institutions, and the moral habits of our people. But it is to be recollected that they happened twenty-seven years ago, in frontier settlements, far distant from the civilized parts of our country. The principal scene of Harpe's atrocities, and of his death, was in that part of Kentucky which lies south of Green River, a vast wilderness, then known by the general name of the *Green River Country*, and containing a few small and thinly scattered settlements—the more dense popula-tion of that state being at that time confined to its northern and eastern parts. The Indians still possessed the country to the south and west. That enormities should sometimes have been practised at these distant spots, cannot be matter of surprise ; the only wonder is that they were so few. The first settlers were a hardy and an honest people ; but they were too few in number, and too widely spread, to be able to create or enforce wholesome civil restraints. Desperadoes, flying from justice, or seeking a secure theatre for the perpetration of crime, might frequently escape discovery, and as often elude or openly defy the arm of justice.

LETTER XVIII.

BACKWOODSMEN—REGULATORS.

It has been objected that such "horrid details" as those contained in my last letter are
not proper for publication ; that " such disgusting sketches of human depravity and barbarism manifest either a vitiated taste or a
total disregard of the morals of the community."
I reply, that whatever tends to develope the
history or character of a people, is a legitimate
subject of public discussion. History, to be
of any value, must be true. It must disclose,
not only the truth, but the whole truth. In
vain would the historian seek this in frail
monuments, vaguely preserved in the uncertain legends of tradition. He must resort to

national records, and to the testimony of writers
contemporary with the events which he attempts
to describe, and if the latter abstain from the
narration of " disgusting sketches of human
depravity and barbarism," history must be cur-
tailed of her most fruitful source of incident,
and men and nations stripped of their boldest
peculiarities. It is perhaps forgotten, that
" depravity and barbarism" constitute almost
the sole basis of history, tragedy, and epic song;
that kings and courts are nothing without them;
that they revel amid "the pomp, pride, and circumstance of glorious war ;" that they are the
very elements of faction and revolution ;
and stand forth, in bold relief, in every department of civil subordination. They exist in the
contemplation of every religious, and moral,
and municipal code ; all philosophy detects
them, and all creeds abjure them ; they are the
fruitful cause of disease—the prolific source of
incident; and all nature proclaims that "man
is prone to evil, as the sparks fly upward."
It is to be deplored that such is the fact; but
while crime and folly continue to predomi-
nate in the affairs of men, they will be found

to swell the pages of those who attempt to exhibit correct pictures of human nature.

In describing the American backwoodsmen, a class of men peculiar to our country, I thought it proper to introduce, among other authentic anecdotes, the story of the Harpes. My object was to display, as well the extraordinary sufferings to which the emigrants to the western country were exposed, as the courage with which they met and repelled those hardships. —When we know that the state of Kentucky was settled by the farmers of Virginia and North Carolina, we are at a loss to discover by what process a race of husbandmen were transformed into a bold, adventurous, military people. The toils of the chase, or the mere labour of subduing the forest, were not of themselves calculated to produce these traits of character, without the addition of some other powerful causes. The history of Kentucky is fruitful in interesting events, which awakened the courage and exercised the ingenuity of her citizens, while they implanted that military spirit which is still a conspicuous feature in the character of that patriotic state ; but these, it seems, are forbidden to us, because it has just been found out, that a regard for "the morals of the community" renders it improper to disclose the "barbarism" of the Indian, or the "depravity" of the felon who flies for safety to a frontier. These researches *may*, or they *may not*, manifest "a vitiated taste"—the public will decide that question. In the meantime, if I am to be allowed to speculate upon the peculiarities of my countrymen, I must claim the privilege of managing my case according to my own judgment, holding myself responsible to no other constraints than such as are indicated by a respect for *religion, truth,* and *modesty*. Whenever I shall offend against either of these, by a wilful mis-statement or an idle jest, I shall submit in silence to the censure of public indignation. I desire to be an author no longer than I can combine the cheerfulness of wit with the morality of a christian, and the courtesy of good-breeding. Without these, a writer is a pest worse than an influenza, a tariff, or a paper-bank.*

---

* These remarks are made in reply to some strictures upon

The manners and institutions of a new people are always curious—presenting the naked outlines of character, the first rudiments of civilization, and all the simple elements of society. In New England, the *fathers* contended successfully with the savage and the climate; they made laws, burned witches, prohibited kissing, and knocked their beer-barrels on the head for *working* on the Sabbath. They had many simple fashions, and queer ways, which have vanished with their witches and their blue laws. They were not so military in their habits, as their prototypes in the west; because, though equally brave and enterprising, they were more industrious, more frugal, and less mercurial in their temperament. Religion was with them a powerful spring of action, and discouraged all wars except those of self-defence. The social and moral virtues, the sciences and arts, were cherished and respected; and there were many roads to office and to eminence, which were safer and more

one of these letters, which appeared in a periodical work, and which do not require a more particular notice.

certain, and not less honourable, than the bloody path of warlike achievement.

Kentucky was settled at a period when religious fanaticism had vanished, and when the principles of the revolution, then in full operation, had engendered liberal and original modes of thinking—when every man was a politician, a soldier, and a patriot, ready to make war or to make laws, to put his hand to the plough or to the helm of state, as circumstances might require. They went to a wilderness with all these new notions in their heads, full of ardour, and full of projects, determined to add a new state to the family of republics, at all hazards. With Boon for their file-leader, they resolutely breasted all opposition. The rifle and the axe were incessantly employed. The savage was to be expelled ; the panther, the wolf, and the bear to be exterminated ; the forest to be razed ; houses to be built : and when all this was accomplished, their labours were but commenced. Separated, by an immense wilderness, and by the rugged ridges of the Alleghany mountains, from the older settlements, the transportation of heavy articles was at first impossible, and for many years difficult and expensive. The pioneers, therefore, brought little else with them than their weapons, and their ammunition; those who followed in their footsteps brought cattle, and hogs, and a few articles of immediate necessity, laden upon pack-horses. With no tools but an axe and an augur, the settler built his cabin; with a chimney built of sticks, and a door hung upon wooden hinges, and confined with a wooden latch. Chairs, tables, and bedsteads, were fabricated with the same unwieldy tools. These primitive dwellings are by no means so wretched as their name and their rude workmanship seem to imply. They still constitute the usual residence of the farmers in new settlements, and I have often found them roomy, tight, and comfortable. If one cabin is not sufficient, another, and another is added, until the whole family is accommodated; and thus the homestead of a substantial farmer often resembles a little village. Farming utensils were next to be fabricated, and land to be cleared and fenced; and while all this was carrying on, the new settler had to provide food for his

U

family with his rifle, to look after his stock,
which ranged the woods, exposed to the " wild
varmints," and to " keep a red eye out" for
Indians.   In addition to these more important
matters, it will readily be imagined, that a number of little things would have to be made, and
done, and provided, before the woodsman,
adhering strictly to the system of *home manufacture*, could be " *well fixed*," as their phrase
is ; a man who goes into the woods, as one of
these veterans observed to me, " has *a heap* of
little *fixens* to *study out*, and a great deal of
projecking to do, as well as hard work."

At the close of the revolution the state of
Virginia rewarded her military officers by dona-
tions of land, in the then *district of Kentucky*.
Many of these gentlemen, with others who at
the close of the war found themselves without
employment, emigrated to that country, carrying with them, the courage, skill, and lofty
notions incident to military command.   They
became the leaders in the Indian wars ; and as
bravery is necessarily held in the highest estimation among a people who are exposed to
danger, they soon became the popular men of

the country, and filled many of the civil offices.
The people and the institutions imbibed their
spirit, and the Kentuckians became a chivalrous
people.   Brave and hardy they must have been
from their manner of life ; but we must attribute much of their hospitality, their polish,
and their intelligence to the gentlemen of Virginia, who came to this state in early times,
bringing with them education, wealth, and
talents.

Among the early settlers there was a way of
trying causes, which may perhaps be new to
you. No commentator has taken any notice of
Linch's Law, which was once the *lex loci* of the
frontiers. Its operation was as follows : when
a horse thief, a counterfeiter, or any other desperate vagabond, infested a neighbourhood,
evading justice by cunning, or by a strong arm,
or by the number of his confederates, the
citizens formed themselves into a " *regulating
company,*" a kind of holy brotherhood, whose
duty was to purge the community of its unruly
members. Mounted, armed, and commanded
by a leader, they proceeded to arrest such notorious offenders as were deemed fit subjects of

exemplary justice ; their operations were generally carried on in the night. Squire Birch,
who was personated by one of the party, established his tribunal under a tree in the woods,
and the culprit was brought before him, tried,
and generally convicted ; he was then tied to
a tree, lashed without mercy, and ordered to
leave the country within a given time, under
pain of a second visitation. It seldom happened
that more than one or two were thus punished ;
their confederates took the hint and fled, or
were admonished to quit the neighbourhood.
Neither the justice nor the policy of this practice can be defended, but it was often resorted
to from necessity, and its operation was salutary
in ridding the country of miscreants whom the
law was not strong enough to punish. It was
liable to abuse, and was sometimes abused ; but
in general it was conducted with moderation, and
only exerted upon the basest and most lawless
men. Sometimes the sufferers resorted to courts
of justice for remuneration, and there have been
instances of heavy damages being recovered of
the *regulators*. Whenever a county became
strong enough to enforce the laws, these high-
handed doings ceased to be tolerated.

LETTER XIX.

THE MISSOURI TRAPPER.

THE varied fortunes of those who bear the above cognomen, whatever may be their virtues or demerits, must, upon the common principles of humanity, claim our sympathy, while they cannot fail to awaken admiration. The hardships voluntarily encountered, the privations manfully endured, by this hardy race, in the exercise of their perilous calling, present abundant proofs of those peculiar characteristics which distinguish the American woodsmen. The trackless deserts of Missouri, the innumerable tributary streams of the Mississippi, the fastnesses of the Rocky Mountains, have all been explored by these bold adventurers ; and the great and increasing importance of the Missouri fur trade, is an evidence as well of their numbers, as of their skill and perseverance.

The ingenious author of Robinson Crusoe has shewn, by an agreeable fiction, that man may exist in a desert, without the society or aid of his fellow-creatures, and unassisted by those contrivances of art which are deemed indispensable in a state of civilized society; that nature will supply all his absolute wants; and that his own ingenuity will suggest ways and means of living which are not dreamt of in the philosophy of polished circles. That which the novelist deemed barely possible, and which has always been considered as marvellously incredible by a large portion of his readers, is now daily and hourly reduced to practice in our western forests. Here may be found many a Crusoe, clad in skins, and contentedly keeping "bachelor's hall" in the wild woods, unblessed by the smile of beauty, uncheered by the voice of humanity—without even a "man Friday" for company, and ignorant of the busy world, its cares, its pleasures, or its comforts.

But the solitary wight whose cabin is pitched in the deepest recess of the forest, whose gun supplies his table, and whose dog is his only comrade, enjoys ease and comfort, in comparison with the trapper, whose erratic steps lead him continually into new toils and dangers. Compelled to procure his subsistence by very precarious means from day to day, in those immense regions of wilderness into which he fearlessly penetrates, he is sometimes known to live for a considerable period upon food over which the hungry wolf would pause for a polite interval before carving. The ordinary food of a trapper is corn and buffaloe-tallow; and although his rifle often procures him more dainty viands, he is frequently, on the other hand, forced to devour his peltry and gnaw his moccasins.

An old man arrived at Fort Atkinson in June last, from the Upper Missouri, who was instantly recognized by some of the officers of the garrison, as an individual supposed some time since to have been devoured by a white bear, but more recently reported to have been slain by the Arickara Indians; his name is Hugh Glass. Whether old Ireland, or Scotch-Irish Pennsylvania claims the honour of his nativity,

I have not ascertained with precision, nor do I suppose that the humble fortunes of the hardy adventurer will excite a rivalry on the subject similar to that respecting the birth-place of Homer. The following is his own account of himself, for the last ten months of his perilous career.

He was employed as a trapper by Major Henry, an enterprising gentleman of St. Louis, engaged in the fur-trade, and was attached to his command before the Arickara towns. After the flight of these Indians, the major and his party set out for the Yellow-stone River. Their route lay up the Grand River, and through a prairie country, occasionally interspersed with thickets of brush-wood, dwarf-plum trees, and other shrubs indigenous to a sandy, sterile soil. As these adventurers usually draw their food, as well as their raiment, from Nature's spacious warehouse, it is customary for one or two hunters to precede the party in search of game, that the whole may not be forced at night to lie down supperless. The rifle of Hugh Glass being esteemed as among the most unerring, he was on one occasion detached for supplies. He was a short distance in advance of the party, and forcing his way through a thicket, when a white bear, that had imbedded herself in the sand, arose within three yards of him, and before he could "set his triggers," or turn to retreat, he was seized by the throat and raised from the ground; casting him again upon the earth, his grim adversary tore out a mouth-ful of the cannibal food which had excited her appetite, and retired to submit the sample to her yearling cubs, which were near at hand. The sufferer now made an effort to escape, but the bear immediately returned with a re-inforce-ment, and seized him by the shoulder: she also lacerated his left arm very much, and in-flicted a severe wound on the back of his head. In this second attack the cubs were prevented from participating, by one of the party who had rushed forward to the relief of his comrade. One of the cubs, however, forced the new-comer to retreat into the river, where, standing to the middle in the water, he gave his foe a mortal shot, or to use his own language, " I burst the varment." Meantime the main body of trappers having arrived, advanced to the relief of Glass, and delivered seven or eight shots, so well directed as to terminate hostilities, by dispatching the bear as she stood over her bleeding victim.

Glass was thus providentially snatched from the grasp of the ferocious animal; yet his condition was far from being enviable : he had received several dangerous wounds, his whole body was bruised and mangled, and he lay weltering in his blood, in exquisite torment. To procure surgical aid, now so desirable, was impossible; and to remove the sufferer was equally so; the safety of the whole party, being now in the country of hostile Indians, depended on the celerity of their movements. To remove the lacerated and scarcely breathing Glass, seemed certain death to him—to the rest of the party such a measure would have been fraught with danger. Under these circumstances, Major Henry, by offering an extravagant reward, induced two of his party to remain with the wounded man until he should expire, or recover sufficient strength to bear removal to some of the trading establishments in that country. They remained with their patient five days, when supposing his recovery to be no longer possible, they cruelly abandoned him, taking with them his rifle, shot pouch, and all appliances, leaving him no means of making fire or procuring food. These unprincipled wretches proceeded on the trail of their employer; and when they overtook him, reported that Glass had died of his wounds, and that they had interred him in the best manner possible. They produced his effects in confirmation of their assertions, and readily obtained credence.

But poor Glass was not "a slovenly, unhandsome corpse;" nor was he willing to yield without a struggle to the grim king of terrors. Retaining a slight hold upon life, when he found himself abandoned, he crawled with great difficulty to a spring, which was within a few yards. Here he laid ten days subsisting upon cherries that hung over the spring, and *gruins des bœufs*, or buffaloe-berries, which were within his reach. Acquiring by slow degrees a little strength, he now set off for Fort Kiawa, a trading post, on the Missouri River, about three hundred and fifty miles distant. It required no

ordinary degree of fortitude to crawl to the end
of such a journey, through a hostile country,
without fire-arms, with scarcely strength to
drag one limb after another, and with almost
no other subsistence than wild berries. He had,
however, the good fortune one day to be "in at
the death of a buffaloe calf," which was overtaken and slain by a pack of wolves. He permitted the assailants to carry on the war, until no
signs of life remained in their victim, and then
interfered and took possession of the "*fatted
calf;*" but as he had no means of striking fire,
we may infer that he did not make a very
prodigal use of the veal thus obtained. With
indefatigable industry, he continued to crawl
until he reached Fort Kiawa.

Before his wounds were entirely healed, the
chivalry of Glass was awakened, and he joined
a party of five *engagés,* who were bound, in a
piroque, to Yellow Stone River. The primary
object of this voyage was declared to be the
recovery of his arms, and vengeance on the
recreant who had robbed and abandoned him in
his hour of peril. When the party had ascended to within a few miles of the old Mandan

village, our trapper of hair-breadth 'scapes, landed for the purpose of proceeding to Tilton's Fort at that place, by a nearer route than that of the river.   On the following day, all the companions of his voyage were massacred by the Arickara Indians.   Approaching the fort with some caution, he observed two squaws whom he recognised as Arickaras, and who, discovering him at the same time, turned and fled. This was the first intelligence which he obtained of the fact, that the Arickaras had taken post at the Mandan village, and he at once perceived the danger of his situation.   The squaws were not long in rallying the warriors of the tribe, who immediately commenced the pursuit. Suffering still under the severity of his recent wounds, the poor fugitive made but a feeble essay at flight, and his enemies were within rifle shot of him, when two Mandan mounted warriors rushed forward and seized him.   Instead of despatching their prisoner, as he had anticipated, they mounted him on a fleet horse, which they had brought out for that purpose, and carried him into Tilton's Fort without injury.

The same evening, Glass crept out of the fort,

and after travelling thirty-eight days alone, and through the country of hostile Indians, he arrived at Henry's establishment.

Finding that the trapper he was in pursuit of had gone to Fort Atkinson, Glass readily consented to be the bearer of letters for that post, and accordingly left Henry's Fort on the Big Horn River, on the 29th of February, 1824. Four men accompanied him : they travelled across to Powder River, which empties itself into the Yellow Stone, below the mouth of the Horn. They pursued their route up the Powder to its source, and thence across to the Platte. Here they constructed skin boats, and descended in them to the lower end of *Les Côtes Noirs*, (the Black Hills), where they discovered thirty-eight lodges of Arickara Indians. This was the encampment of *Gray-eye's* band. That chief had been killed in the attack of the American troops upon his village, and the tribe was now under the command of *Langue de Biche* (Elk's Tongue.) This warrior came down, and invited our little party ashore, and by many professions of friendship, induced them to believe him to be sincere. Glass had once

resided with this *tonguey* old politician during a
long winter, had joined him in the chase, and
smoked his pipe, and cracked many a bottle by
the genial fire of his wigwam; and when he
landed, the savage chief embraced him with the
cordiality of an old friend. The whites were
thrown off their guard, and accepted an invitation to smoke in the Indian's lodge. While
engaged in passing the hospitable pipe, a small
child was heard to utter a suspicious scream.
Glass looked towards the door of the lodge, and
beheld the squaws of the tribe bearing off the
arms and other effects of his party. This was
a signal for a general movement; the guests
sprang from their seats, and fled with precipi-
tation, pursued by their treacherous enter-
tainers: the whites ran for life: the red warriors for blood. Two of the party were overtaken and put to death: one of them within a
few yards of Glass, who had gained a point of
rocks unperceived, and lay concealed from the
view of his pursuers. Versed in all the arts of
border warfare, our adventurer was enabled to
practice them in the present crisis with such
success, as to baffle his blood-thirsty enemies;

and he remained in his lurking place until the search was abandoned in despair. Breathing once more a free air, he sallied forth under cover of the night, and resumed his line of march towards Fort Kiawa. The buffaloe calves at that season of the year, were generally but a few days old; and as the country through which he travelled was abundantly stocked with them, he found it no difficult task to overtake one as often as his appetite admonished him to task his speed for that purpose. "Although," said he, "I had lost my rifle and all my *plunder,* I felt quite rich, when I found my knife, flint, and steel in my shot pouch. These little fixens," added he, "make a man feel right *peart,* when he is three or four hundred miles *from any body* or *any place*—all alone among the *painters* and wild *varments.*"

A journey of fifteen days brought him to Fort Kiawa. Thence he descended to Fort Atkinson, at the Council Bluffs, where he found his old traitorous acquaintance in the garb of a private soldier. This shielded the delinquent from chastisement. The commanding officer at the post ordered his rifle to be restored, and the veteran trapper was furnished with such other appliances—or *fixens*, as he would term them—as put him in plight again to take the field.   This appeased the wrath of Hugh Glass, whom my informant left, astounding, with his wonderful narration, the gaping rank and file of the garrison.

LETTER XX.

EMIGRATION.

HAVING in my former letters endeavoured to sketch a faint outline of the character and sufferings of the first settlers of this country, I shall now give you some traits of a less hardy race, its more recently acquired inhabitants. Between those persons, and the subjects of my present communication, there exist these marked distinctions; namely :—the first were a peculiar class of men, accustomed to danger and privations; the latter are persons taken from all the various grades of civilized society; the former came to conquer a country, the latter to enjoy it; the former came from the southern, the latter from the eastern and middle states ; the former took possession of Kentucky ; the latter are crowding to Ohio, Indiana, and Illinois. I am aware that it is impossible to do justice to this subject within the compass of a letter ; but I feel also the danger of entering too minutely upon a theme which presents a vast variety of interesting features. To say nothing of the mighty revolution which a score of years has produced in this wonderful country —of the extensive regions which have been civilized, or of the sublime reflections excited by the establishment of states and governments, there are a thousand minor traits in the scenes which I have witnessed—pictures of domestic life and individual fortune, which present new and affecting views of human nature. If the miserable victims of penury, alone, changing only the scene of distress, had sought refuge in these solitudes, or if none but the greedy worshippers of mammon had braved the fury of the blast, and the gloom of the wilderness, a single stroke of the pen might display the merits and the fortunes of all. The hacknied tale of virtue in distress, would draw for the former the common tribute of a tear ; while the latter would be abandoned without commiseration, to the just rewards of overweening avarice.

But the mighty stream has not emanated from a single fountain—it comes compounded of various elements, flowing from a thousand sources, mingling and combining their discordant materials into one great and living mass. Industry sends her sun-brown children, avarice her minions, ambition her aspirants, and sorrow her heavily laden offspring. Never, since the days when a romantic religious enthusiasm allured all ages, sexes, and conditions, to the shrine of a favourite saint, has the world witnessed such party-coloured hordes, peacefully pursuing a common path to a common destination.

This subject was forcibly presented to my mind, a few years ago, during a journey over the Alleghany mountains; and as the lonely scenes among which these impressions were made upon my memory, are peculiarly fitted to exemplify the toils, and to gvie a tinge of the picturesque to the adventures of the emigrants whom I there encountered, you must linger with me here for a few moments.

The traveller who crosses the stupendous chain of mountains which form a dividing line between the two great sections of our country, often pauses to ponder on the deep gloom and savage wildness presented to his eye. Nature seems to have reserved these strong fastnesses to herself, as a last retreat from the encroachments of art. Her precarious sway over the valley and the plain, is incessantly assailed by the unwearied arm of civilization, which every day despoils some fair portion of her ancient dominion. The rill no longer murmurs in the solitude, nor does the songster alone fill the grove with his melody; the discordant hum of a busy world mingles its hoarse tones with those notes of sweet and native eloquence by which nature speaks to her delighted votaries; the " dappled denizen" of the forest shade has fled, and the forest itself is prostrated by the fierce invaders. But here she sits securely enthroned among her favourite wilds, defended by bulwarks which bid defiance to invasion. Man, the sworn enemy to the fairest works of his Creator, advances to the barrier, and halts; he pauses on the brink of the precipice, mea-

sures with a despairing eye the overhanging
cliff, and retires from the conflict.

No description can convey any adequate
idea of the winding paths, the steep acclivities,
the overhanging cliffs, and dark ravines, with
which these Alpine regions abound—the sublime grandeur of the scenery, or the difficulty
and danger of the roads. At the time of which
I am speaking, the turnpikes, which have since
rendered the passes of the mountains so safe
and easy, were not completed; and if I found
it toilsome in the extreme to accomplish my
journey on horseback, you may conceive the
almost insurmountable difficulties presented
to weary-laden wanderers, encumbered with
waggons and baggage; yet I found these roads
crowded with emigrants of every description,
but the majority were of the poorest class.
Here I would meet a few lusty fellows, trudging
it merrily along; and there a family, more embarrassed, and less cheerful: now a gang of
forty or fifty souls, men, women, and children;
and now a solitary pedestrian, with his oaken
staff, his bottle, and his knapsack; and, once a
day, a stage-load of tired travellers, dragged

heavily towards the west. Sometimes I beheld a gentleman toiling along with a broken-down vehicle, and sometimes encountered the solitary horseman : here I espied the wreck of a carriage, or the remains of a meal; and there the temporary shelter which had protected the benighted stranger. At one time, beside a small stream rushing through a narrow glen, I encountered a party of about fourscore persons, with two or three waggons. They had halted to bait ; the beasts were grazing among the rocks, the men cleaving wood for fires, and boughs to erect a tenement for the hour ; the women cooking or nursing their children, and the rosy boys and girls dabbling in a waterfall. When, from the summit of a mountain, or one of its precipices, where the road wound beneath my feet, appearing at intervals as far as the eye could reach, I beheld one of these large caravans, composed of half-clad beings, of every age and sex, slowly winding up the mountain path, or reclining at mid-day among the rocks, I could compare them only to the gipsy bands, described by foreign novelists.

At one of the most difficult passes of the

mountain I met a cavalcade, whose description will apply to a numerous class ; they were from New England. The senior of the party was a middle-aged man, hale, well built, and decently clad. He was guiding a pair of small, lean, active horses, harnessed to a light waggon, which contained the bedding and provisions of the party, and a few articles of household furniture ; two well-grown, barefoot boys, in homespun shirts and trowsers, held the tail of the waggon, laudably endeavouring to prevent an *upset*, by throwing their weight occasionally to that side which seemed to require ballast, while the father exerted his arms, voice, and whip, in urging forward his ponies. In the rear toiled the partner of his pilgrimage, conducting, like John Rodgers' wife, " nine small children and one at the breast," and exhibiting, in her own person and those of her offspring, ample proof, that whatever might be the character of the land to which they were hastening, that which they had left was not deficient in health or fruitfulness. Nor must I omit to mention a chubby boy of six years old, who by sundry falls and immersions, had acquired the hue of the soil from head to foot, and though now trudging knee-deep in the mire, was craunching an apple with the most entire composure. They had reached the summit of the mountain just as I overtook them, and as they halted to rest, I checked my horse to observe them. As they stretched their eyes forward over the interminable prospect, they were wrapped in silent wonder. As far as the vision could extend there was nothing to intercept it; beneath our feet lay mountains, and vallies, and forests, and rivers, all of which must be passed before these

> " Sad unravellers
> Of the mazes to the mountain's top,"

could reach the land of promise, which they imagined they could now dimly discern in the distant horizon. They looked back with a kind of shuddering triumph at what they had accomplished; they looked forward with a trembling hope at what was to come. I thought I could see in their faces regret, hope, fear, resignation—but they spoke cheerfully, and expressed no dissatisfaction; and after answering their inquiries as to their route onward, I left them. Tired souls! they have, probably, long ere this, surmounted their fatigues, and found a happy home in a land of plenty, where, surrounded with fat pigs and fat children, they enjoy the only true *otium cum dignitate* ; while I, delving among the labyrinths of the *law*, find mazes more intricate, and steeps more arduous, than the winding paths of the mountain.

The foreigners whom I met were in much worse circumstances than our own citizens. These arrive on our shores in a destitute condition, and undertake the journey without money enough to accomplish half the distance, and some without a cent to pay their entrance, confiding in the protection of Heaven and the benefactions of the charitable. This confidence is not so often deceptive as might be expected, for an American is never seen to turn a houseless wanderer from his door, or to refuse a morsel to the hungry. It is surprising to see to what a dreary plight some of these adventurers are reduced by their poverty or improvidence ; and yet many of them will trudge along with light hearts and empty purses, apparently forgetful of the past and regardless of the future. At Pittsburgh, where the emigrants, generally, embark on the Ohio, they may be seen in larger numbers than at any other place; and here may be remarked, not only their number, but, in some degree, their various characters, and as various expectations. Some arrive with furniture, farming utensils, and servants, and push forward, confident in their ability to overcome every obstacle; some come burthened with large families, and but little worldly gear; and others, happy at such a time in their " single blessedness," come alone, errant knights, leaving all their cares behind them. Upon observing these motley collections, I have been reminded of the invitation in a camp-meeting song which I have heard, and which I think is about as follows :

" Come hungry, come thirsty, come ragged, come bare,
Come filthy, come lousy, come just as you are."

For, to be brief, here you see all sorts of folks crowding to the west.

Those who are driven by misfortune from their homes, go like exiles from the land to which fond recollection attaches a thousand charms, to a wilderness which fancy clothes with a thousand terrors. Every sympathy is awakened, and every tender feeling thrilled with anguish, when they exchange the comforts of society, the scenes of their youth, and the friends of their hearts, for the nameless and unknown difficulties which appear in the dark perspective. They dream of interminable forests, and pestilential swamps, and at every step fancy themselves surrounded by noxious vermin and beasts of prey. Thus, anticipating no good and fearing every evil, they go into banishment with sorrowful hearts. But there is a more sanguine class of emigrants, to whom a different picture is presented. They have been allured by interest or ambition, or led by choice, to a new country, and hope arrays their future abodes with every charm. An *El Dorado* has been described to them, or they have created it, in which men are to be wooed to their happiness as a maiden to the bridal, and their only care is to determine with what grace they will accept the guerdon. The old men are to be blessed with wealth, the young men

with honour, and the girls with husbands—and,
I suppose, with wealth, and honour, and pleasure into the bargain; and, to crown all, the
good folks of the west will feel so delighted
and so flattered by their advent, that they will
crowd about them like the friends of Job, and
every one will give them " an ear-ring and a
piece of gold!"

All these are deceived, as well the desponding as the enthusiastic. The advantages of the
western country consist in the great fertility of
the soil, the profusion of all the products of
nature, whether of the animal, vegetable, or
mineral kingdom, the cheapness of lands, and
the *newness* of the country, which affords *room*
and *opportunity* for enterprise. These, together
with its commercial advantages, the total ex-
emption from all taxes and political burthens,
and the comparatively small portion of labour
requisite to procure the *necessaries* of life, certainly render this a desirable home. But they
who, like Ortogrul of Basra, desire the golden
stream to be quick and violent, will like him
discover a dry and dusty channel, and will
learn that slow and persevering industry is not

less necessary here than elsewhere. Honours
are the reward of personal popularity, which,
we have been told, " may be gained without
merit and lost without a fault," and in this
respect the western hemisphere differs little
from the rest of the world. Popular arts are
the same in every country ; but it is certain
that few here are raised to eminent public
stations without a long and intimate acquaintance with the people. In the west there is no
jealousy or unfriendliness to strangers, who are
generally received with open arms, and treated
with kindness and respect ; but political honours
are more sparingly bestowed, and are seldom
lavished upon foreigners, who, whatever may
be their pretensions, can hardly be supposed to
know or to feel the interests of the country.

The desponding emigrant, on the other hand,
is agreeably surprised at finding every plain,
substantial comfort which a reasonable man can
wish : and though he discovers no attempt at
luxury or style, he sees hospitality, plenty, and
intelligence. Instead of a vast wilderness, he
finds large settlements, which, though thinly
scattered, are now sufficiently dense to afford

the comforts and civilities of life, to ensure pro_
tection and to enforce municipal regulations.

Of all people the English are most pro-
vokingly disappointed ; the Irish, Dutch, and
French amalgamate easily with our people,
adopt our habits, and live happily among us.
But not so John Bull : this honest gentleman,
as he is generally pleased to style himself, has
always been famed for an inordinate share of
credulity, so that, notwithstanding his prejudices
against America, he is easily persuaded that
gold is to be ploughed up in our fields and
rubies plucked from the trees. He forgets that
the days of Columbus and Cortes have gone
by, and that Mexico and Peru are not within
our boundaries. With these views he sets out
from one of the Atlantic cities, and soon gets
into " lots of trouble." In the first place, Mr.
Bull is used to being told that he is obstinate,
whimsical, and fond of having his own way,
and he is determined not to detract from the
national character ; he will, therefore, receive
no advice as to his route or mode of travelling,
and consequently adopts the most inconvenient
vehicle, takes the worst road, and stops at the

most indifferent houses. He has resolved that he must have tea and rolls in the morning, and tea and toast in the evening, and roast beef for dinner, all of which must be prepared in a particular manner; and if he happen to be thwarted in these important matters, he as resolutely determines not to eat a mouthful until compelled by hunger, nor to pay his fare until obliged by the law. Then he wears a fantastical, fur jockey-cap, which he is advised to exchange for a covering better suited to the climate; but he persists in having his own way, and although his face is scorched and blistered by the sun, he adheres to the fur cap as tenaciously as if it was the *magna charta*. Nor is he less attached to his dandy surtout and other dandy habiliments; he cannot be convinced that what may be a suitable dress in " Lunnun," may be very unfit to travel in, and he rather submits to be tortured and pinched until he is sore, than to leave off the finery which is worn *at 'ome*, and which he fondly imagines will entitle him to singular honour, by distinguishing him from the natives— the odious, vile Americans! among whom, however, he is pleased to live, if he can be said to be pleased, who is always on the fret. All this is of no consequence to any body but himself; but unluckily, John is not satisfied with having *his own way*, but is displeased that others claim the same privilege, and perseveringly finds fault with every thing he sees, hears, smells, tastes, or touches. Then he has an odd propensity for *quizzing the natives*, and many a box on the ear and tweak of the nose this may cost the poor gentleman on his hapless way; till he finds out at last, that it is just as foolish to meddle with the folks on shore, as to be fingering about their " striped bunting" at sea. His opinions are as singular as his manners; he is a great politician,

> " Sits up till midnight with his host,
> Talks politics, and gives the toast :"

and being accustomed at home to join church and state, he seldom fails to give religion a side-blow in discussing his political tenets. If he happen to be a monarchist, he finds few associates; if a radical, he disgusts his hearers by his utter disregard of order, law, decency, and virtue : and, in either case, he fails not to ridicule our institutions and revile our government,

Y

Arrived at the end of the journey, he seeks an
English settlement, avoids all intercourse with
"the natives," quarrels with his countrymen,
engages in a law-suit, spends his money, and
finding that he cannot subsist without labour,
curses the country, and gets drunk daily. In a
short time he returns home, fully competent to
the task of edifying the British public in relation to American politics, history, and literature.
He writes a book full of wonders, and dangers,
about cataracts in the Ohio, slaves in New
England, alligators in the Hudson, and bare-
footed belles in Philadelphia. Mr. Quarterly Reviewer pronounces him a very clever traveller,
and John Bull at home gapes and wonders at
the " hair breadth 'scapes" of John Bull abroad.

In descending the river, three different descriptions of boats are at the service of the
voyager—the steam-boat, the keel, and the flat
bottom. The steam-boats, which are numerous,
are strong, beautiful, and swift, and are provided with excellent accommodations ; but these
can only run when the water is high, and this
mode of conveyance is in some cases too expensive for the circumstances of the emigrant.

In either of these events, the other boats are resorted to. The keel is a long, sharp vessel, drawing but little water; when loaded, the hull is nearly all immersed, but there is a deck or roof, about six feet high, covered on all sides so as to exclude the weather, and leaving only a passage of about a foot wide, which is called the running board, along the gun-wale, and a small space at the stem and stern. This deck, or roof, affords an admirable lounge in pleasant weather, but at other times the passenger is limited to very narrow bounds below; the oars, which are placed at the bow, are from eight to twelve in number, and are used only in descending the river. By means of these the boat is propelled at the rate of two or three miles an hour faster than the current, which has an average velocity of about three miles. The oars are plied during the day, and at night the boat is suffered to float, with a man at the helm, and one at the bow to look out, except in those parts of the river where the navigation is difficult, and where they always lay by for daylight. A hundred miles in twenty-four hours is accomplished with ease. In ascending the stream these boats are propelled with poles, and the passage is very tedious, seldom averaging more than from ten to twenty miles per day.

The flat-bottom boat is a mere raft, with sides and a roof; but it is more roomy and convenient than the keel, if well built and tight, as indeed they mostly are. An immense oar is placed on the roof on each side near the bow, (which has given these boats the nick-name of " broad horns,") and another at the stern. These are used only to direct the course of the flat, which is allowed to float with the current, and thus she pursues her voyage, like man on his earthly pilgrimage, to that undiscovered country from whose bourne no traveller of her species ever returns ; for, being calculated to stem the current, she is useless after she has reached her destination, except as so much lumber.

Well, and when the emigrant has reached his journey's end, what then? Why then, my dear Sir, he very often finds that he had better have staid at home. Labour, labour, labour,

hard, heavy, incessant labour, is the lot of him
who proclaims war against the forest ; but the
victory is certain, and the conqueror's reward
is rich and ample.

LETTER XXI.

POPULAR SUPERSTITIONS.

EVERY nation has its peculiar superstitions, which are often so closely interwoven with the feelings and prejudices of a whole people, as to form a part of the national character, and to exert a powerful influence, as well upon their political and religious institutions, as on their social intercourse. So intensely do these feelings operate upon the human mind, that to them may be traced bloody wars and mighty revolutions—to them thrones have been indebted for support, and churches for power—and they have produced many of those mournful tragedies in domestic life, which shock humanity, and fatally arrest the progress of moral refinement. The wheel

of Juggernaut, and the dungeons of the Inquisition, are terrific monuments of this truth ;
and the page of history unfolds but too many
instances in which vices of state have been
sanctified, in the popular estimation, by a blind,
infatuated reverence for the *sacred persons* of the
misdoers. When we see that, in all ages, and
throughout almost the whole of the habitable
globe, that *the few* have cruelly oppressed the
many—when we know that a people have but to
will their freedom to obtain it, and that their
happiness, and moral improvement, depend
entirely upon their own desire of knowledge,
and practice of virtue—we readily perceive
how effectually ignorance may be deceived by
art, how chains may be rivetted, and darkness
perpetuated, by delusion and prejudice.

But there are superstitions, of a more innocent character, which are cherished with equal
tenacity, while they awaken no serious appre-
hension in the breast of the patriot or the
christian. These are such as are confined to
local objects, or humble pursuits, which exert
a quiet influence over untutored minds, and
operate chiefly upon rustic manners, employ-

ments, and festivities. To the philosopher,
these have afforded matter of curious investigation; to the poet and novelist they have
suggested the finest incidents which adorn the
page of fiction. We have seen how copiously
the *author of Waverley* has drawn from this
source, and by combining the traditions of his
country with the inventions of his own genius,
has woven the most splendid literary fabrics
which have appeared to feast the reason or
delight the fancy of any age. That the eloquence of the pulpit is seldom, if ever, employed upon this subject, is surprising : for
although the lesser grade of superstitions of
which I now speak, can neither prostrate the
Cross nor endanger government, they certainly
pervert the understanding, and weaken the efficacy of religion. Supernatural events can only
be brought about by unearthly agents. To suppose that the Almighty superintends the operations of a conjuror, or the working of a spell,
would be a sacrilege so gross as to shock the
most careless mind; and to acknowledge the
existence and exercise of such powers in the
prince of darkness, would be to encourage the

substitution of unlawful appeals to the enemy of
mankind, for an humble reliance in the goodness of Providence, and a steady exertion of
our own faculties. A belief in the efficacy of
charms, and in the working of miracles upon
trivial occasions, is alike inconsistent with
human reason and divine revelation. The
regular operation of causes and effects has
never been interrupted, except to display the
power of the Deity, and to advance the great,
ultimate interests of man. It should therefore
be the business of the divine to teach an ex-
clusive reliance upon Him, and to expose the
fallacy of any belief which is not founded upon
reason or revelation. To believe the existence
of concurrent power elsewhere, is to disbelieve
the omnipotence of God.

The American people have no national, and
but few local superstitions. The general diffusion of intelligence, has left no rank of society in absolute ignorance; and we find few
individuals in that state of intellectual degrada-
tion which pervades the lower orders throughout a large portion of the globe. Almost all
have arrived at that degree of refinement, at

least, which awakens the mind to inquiry, and brings it within the reach and influence of knowledge. Many have the desire, and few are without the means, of literary improvement; all can read, while the multiplicity of news-papers, and the cheapness of books, give to all the opportunity of attaining mental acquire-ments. Nor has the heartless fastidiousness of pride erected in our country those artificial barriers which proclaim eternal separation be-tween the rich and the poor, the ignorant and the learned, and which debar the individual of few accomplishments from the conversation of him who has many. There are certain natural divi-sions, which will invariably take place in every society : the laborious and the prudent will avoid the dissipated and the extravagant; the rational, the thinking, and the moral part of the community, will shun the contagion of licentiousness and vice; the delicacy of refine-ment will not endure the familiarity of its opposite; and the poor will never intrude upon the pleasures of the rich. Youth and gallantry will crowd to the levee of beauty—learning to the resorts of science—and ambition to active scenes of human exertion. Politically, and civilly, we are all equals, and we are in the habit of asserting this truth upon all suitable occasions; but in the ordinary enjoyment of social intercourse, every man seeks his companions among those who are his equals in fortune or in intellectual endowment—those in whom he can recognise a community of taste and feeling. Circles are thus created, upon much more rational and less arbitrary principles than those of hereditary rank, and which equally answer the purposes of their institution. But we erect no impassable barriers; to none do we say, "thus far shalt thou come, and no farther." The genius of the republican compact, the habits of the people, the diffusion of knowledge, the rational, liberal, and acute modes of thinking which prevail, all forbid this. A door is left open to the ambition which would rise, or the humility that would condescend; through this curiosity may sometimes gaze, but politeness and decency seldom fail to prevent intrusion. The man would be ridiculed who should *assert* a superiority over his fellow citizens; but he is, tacitly and freely,

invested with all the advantages of any adven-
titious superiority, which he is content to receive with modesty, and enjoy with moderation.
Thus, although there certainly are degrees
and bounds, which define the ordinary intercourse of society, they are such as are established by inclination, good sense, and taste,
and which, upon proper occasions, may be
overstepped without offence.   The learned and
the ignorant come frequently into contact : the
poor man finds his way to the tables of the rich,
while the latter enjoys the welcome repast in
the dwellings of the laborious sons of industry.
Those on either side who choose to keep aloof,
can always do so ; but that choice is seldom
made.   This occasional intercourse, between
persons so apparently different in character,
and so widely separated by fortune, arises from
a liberal concession on both sides, and it prevents that bitterness of feeling which is apt to
be engendered where distinctions of rank are
rigidly observed, and where scorn on the one
hand, and hatred upon the other, poisons the
enjoyments of both parties.   In all countries
there must be occasions of promiscuous assem-

blage; "a cat may look at a king," a peasant will sometimes rub against a lord, and at such a meeting, the gentleman who is in the habit of spurning his inferiors, defends himself in sullen dignity from the contamination which he fears, or the malignity which he is conscious of having excited; while the inferior recoils in dislike, or triumphs in his temporary equality. But where no offence has been given, there is nothing to resent; where dignity is not thought to be in danger, there is no necessity of vigilance; and we meet, when we must meet, with frankness. By these collisions, the acquirements of a few are partially communicated to many. Correct estimates of human nature are thus formed, by those who see men in so many different grades. Prejudice and superstition are removed, as well by the general spread of intelligence, and the consequent invigoration of the intellect, as by the intimate acquaintance of all the members of a community with each other. Where so much of real life is seen, but little room is left for the operation of fancy; and if prejudice be a false estimate of men and things, it can seldom exist where

men are familiarly seen, and things freely can-
vassed.

Nor is there any thing in a new country congenial to the existence of those fairy creations
which bewilder the mind in older communities.
Superstition disports in the misty clouds of
antiquity; she revels in dilapidation, and finds
faithful chroniclers in tottering old men and
toothless women. Castles and dungeons in
ruin, are the chosen abodes of those aristocratic
elves, who choose to be the successors of none
but lords and ladies. Brownies, indeed, haunt
the farm-yard, and nestle in the attic chamber
of the cottage; but they are sure to infest an
old-fashioned edifice, which has whilom sheltered
a marvellously learned schoolmaster or an
obnoxious reforming minister. Fairies, I grant,
may be sought in any glen which is picturesque
and lonely, but they are seldom found except
where melodious shepherds tune their pipes, and
beautiful shepherdesses dance upon the green.
Of all the elfin race, these surely exhibit
the purest taste; and if I were fated to revisit
this earth in an ethereal form, I should choose,
in the character of a fairy, to view the sports of

innocence, and listen to the tales of love. The whole goblin fraternity are *filii nullius*, and derive their character from the obscurity of their origin ; like the common law they must have existed " time whereof the memory of man runneth not to the contrary,"—give them a creator or a birth-day, and they perish. The American Indians had few superstitions; we have no account of aboriginal ghosts or copper-coloured brownies. We have acquired no *incorporeal hereditaments* of this description by descent from our predecessors ; and I am very sure that none came in with Penn, or landed with the fathers at Boston. The latter are said to have imported a few choice witches ; but these were kept in order by the salutary provisions of the *blue-laws*, and the increase of them restrained by prudent enactments. From all this I infer, that our new world has no supernatural inhabitants, indigenous or exotic—nor does our country offer any induce-ments to the influx of foreigners of this des-cription. We have no castles mouldering into ruin, no enchanted forests, nor deserted man-sions. Whatever hospitality we might feel

inclined to shew to the inhabitants of the other
world, is effectually repressed by the absence of
accommodations suited to the state of ethereal
beings. Our whole territory does not present a
dilapidated turret, or an unfrequented gallery—
not a hole or corner, fit for a decent ghost to be
seen in—none that a ghost of any spirit would
condescend to infest. We have no subterranean passages, except the *saltpetre caves* in
Kentucky, and a few caverns, similar to that in
which General Putnam slew the she-wolf. We
have heard of *gnomes*,

"That haunt in dark gold mines;"

but they must be grovelling spirits indeed who
would burrow in "villainous saltpetre," or
consort with beasts of prey. No respectable
and truly aristocratic ghost would put up with
a log cabin ; our modern brick and frame
houses are too airy, too ephemeral, for the
sombre taste of such *grave* personages ; and
he would be a dauntless spirit who would infest
the woods whose echoes are daily awakened by
the rifle and the axe, and whose shades are
trod by backwoodsmen, who would as soon

scalp a ghost, if a ghost could be scalped, as they would shoot a panther or an Indian.

I could add forty other reasons for the absence of popular superstitions; but as an eminent judge has declared from the bench, that one reason, if a good one, is as good as forty, I shall withhold the remainder. The poet may deplore a state of things so unfriendly to his creative art, but those who enjoy the blessings of a comfortable fireside and a warm bed, will not join him in regretting the absence of goblins, who would intrude upon the choicest pleasures of life—especially as the expression of such regret would savour rather too much of the sentimental grief of the heroine, Cherubina, who sighed, and wept, and bewailed her hard fortune in having been born in honest wedlock, without a doubt, a mystery, or a stain upon her origin, to render her *miserable* and *interesting*.

But to believe us entirely destitute of these vagaries of fancy, would be to suppose us a nation of philosophers, coldly believing only what reason as coldly teaches. A moderate

z

degree of credulity is necessary to our happiness, for if we believe nothing but what may be demonstrated, we must reject much which mankind have by common consent agreed to receive. Scepticism may be carried to excess, as well as credulity; and it requires more clearness of discrimination than is given to most men, to know exactly where to draw the line.

You, my friend, without doubt, experienced in your infancy that kind solicitude to which all of us are so deeply indebted—that tender care which dried your tears by congealing their fountains with horror, which purchased your obedience by ingenious deceptions, or enforced it by fearful threatenings. In common with the rest of us, you have often nestled in thrilling anguish under the bed-clothes in the firm conviction that some demon hovered around in waiting to seize your unlucky nose in his red-hot pincers, the moment it should peep from it concealment. When the cock crowed at midnight, you were assured that some one who heard it would expire before dawn, and have lain awake in fearful anxiety, until the morning

note of the vigilant bird proclaimed that you
were not the victim. Your infant mind was
instructed in the unerring omen of the death-
watch; you were advised of the danger of
fracturing looking-glasses, and of the momen-
tous consequences of being followed by a
strange black cat. You probably would yet
raise your hand reluctantly to kill a cricket, and
cannot avoid a feeling of self gratulation at the
discovery that you have unwittingly worn a
garment with the wrong side out. These
obligations we sometimes repay to our instruc-
tors, by amusing the imbecility of old age with
similar fictions; the counterfeit coin is imposed
upon the original fabricator, and they who
invented horrors to answer a momentary purpose, die in the full belief of their own inventions. For my own part, I look back upon my
infancy with pain; the tales which astonished
and alarmed my imagination are still vividly
impressed upon my memory; hours and nights
of fear and anguish are freshly remembered
as the events of yesterday; and I cannot think
of a chambermaid, or a nurse, without some

gloomy associations of spectres, raw heads and bloody bones. Such superstitions are current all the world over, and I but mention them to draw the distinction between them, and such as are of local origin.

Perhaps, as there is no professorship in any of our medical colleges for the instruction of *faith doctors,* you may be unacquainted with this branch of the healing art. Yet there are those among your countrymen who prefer faith to physic, and would sooner risk their lives upon the virtue of a spell, than trust them to the skill of a Wistar or a Rush. Your *faith doctor* is one who practices without diploma, and vanquishes disease without drug or lancet; who neither nauseates the palate, nor mars the fair proportions of his patient. Every thing is accomplished by the potency of a charm, which is inoperative unless the patient has entire confidence in its efficacy, and thence arises the appellation of *faith* doctor. The practice of these gentlemen and ladies—for this art is confined to no sex—is as various as their persons, each one having a particular set of remedies, in the use of which the happy possessor is independent of the rest of the faculty, and which he is long enabled to preserve to his own use and behoof, in consequence of the secrecy which he imposes upon his patient. Females, proverbial as they are for the opposite propensity, preserve with inviolable fidelity the hidden mysteries of the faith doctor.

A *seventh son* is a faith doctor in virtue of his birth. His knowledge being intuitive, he may commence practice at the tenderest years : nor can he ever after acquire any additional skill from the disclosures of others, as he already possesses all that others might communicate. But to give full force and virtue to this charm, it is necessary that seven sons should be born in succession : should an unlucky daughter intervene, blasted are all the hopes of the expecting family ; the seventh lad comes into the world with the same dull perceptions as his fellow men.

Persons who have never seen their fathers, derive from that circumstance great medical skill ; and thus, what would otherwise be deplored as a misfortune, becomes a benefit, and a

posthumous child is compensated for the loss of
a parent by the gain of a lucrative pofession.
An infant born in the absence of his paternal
ancestor, is certainly placed in a whimsical
dilemma. Two alternatives are presented, either
of which is unpleasant enough : a parent or a
profession must be lost ; he has the promise of
future eminence under conditions like those
of a penal bond, which the return of his father
is to render " null and void, otherwise it is to be
and remain in full force and virtue."

The *Indian doctor* is also held in high estimation. To sustain this character, it is by no
means necessary to inherit the aboriginal blood ;
though this is certainly an advantage, and a
genuine Indian is always to be preferred. But
it is admitted, that any one who has ever been in
the Indian country, or who speaks an Indian
dialect, or who has ever seen or heard of an
Indian, may well, particularly if of a swarthy
complexion, be an Indian doctor. The peculiar
characteristic of this sect is their knowledge of
plants, " from the cedar tree that is in Lebanon,
even unto the hyssop that springeth out of the
wall ;" and of these their materia medica is

composed. I am inclined to believe, however, that the botanical knowledge thus assumed, is not always possessed, and, if possessed, is superfluous, as there is reason to believe, that in the hands of an Indian doctor, one plant is as efficacious as another.

Another class of privileged beings are *water witches.* These are persons who, by the aid of a small forked hazel rod, profess to be able to discover subterranean fountains. The feats of these persons are somewhat surprising, and have caused a great deal of speculation. Persons desiring to sink wells in situations where it is doubtful whether water can be found, resort to the water-witch, who after passing over the ground with his rod, points out the spot, and names the depth at which a vein may be struck ; and, strange as it may appear, their predictions are often verified. I have known an instance in which three of those persons, strangers to each other, have at different times, and without any privity or concert, selected the same spot, and named the identical number of feet, at which water was afterwards found : from which it would seem that their operations were founded upon some general rule. It is probable that long practice has enabled them to ascertain the presence of water, by the appearance of the country, the quality of the soil, and the growth of the vegetation.

Many of the hunters in this country believe that their rifles can be *charmed*, so as to prevent them from killing game. There are persons who profess to impose, and to remove this spell.

The moon is a wonderful worker of miracles, and never was an enchanter worshipped by so numerous a host of implicit believers. Philosophers assign to her the regulation of tides, and rustics endow her with absolute supremacy over the land. No saint in the calendar was ever consulted so often, or with such entire faith, as the man in the moon; his picture, if it be his, which displays itself as a frontispiece in all our almanacks, surrounded by the ram and the bull, and other mysterious confederates, is more frequently perused than the choicest production of the Italian schools. But it seems that the *man* is not really in the moon, but the moon in the man, and that, like the gout, she flies from limb to limb, and from one part of his body to another, observing, however, the most punctilious regularity in her migrations. By these changes all farming operations are regulated ; seed is sown, fences are made, and children weaned, when the moon is propitious ; and, by the same rule, I presume that a maiden who should be courted when the *sign was in the heart*, would melt sooner than at any other period. A dancing master, I suppose, makes his harvest when the "chaste cold" luminary is in the heels, the lawyer when she mounts to the head, and the merchant when she settles in the neighbourhood of the pocket ; for my part, I am convinced that at this very moment she is snugly nestled in the brain, for mine will yield nothing but mere moonshine.

LETTER XXII.

TALES OF TRAVELLERS.

A WEARY way-farer, who journeyed through Ohio a few years ago, illustrated his remarks upon the badness of the roads, by relating the following *curious fact.*   He was floundering through the mire, as many an honest gentleman flounders through life, getting along with difficulty, but still getting along ; sometimes wading to the saddle-girth in water, sometimes clambering over logs, and occasionally plunged in a quagmire.   While carefully picking his way by a spot more miry than the rest, he espied a man's hat, a very creditable beaver, lying with the crown upwards in the mud, and as he approached, was not a little startled to see it *move.* This happened in a dismal swamp, where the cypress waved its melancholy branches over the

dark soil, and the frogs croaked as mournfully
as they did of old, under the reign of King
Stork, and as incessantly as if an influenza had
invaded their borders; and our traveller's flesh
began to creep at beholding a hat move without the agency of a head. "When the brains
are out the *head* will die," thought he, "and
when the head is out, the hat, by the same rule,
should receive its *quietus*." Not being very superstitious, and determined to penetrate the
mystery, the solitary rider checked his nag, and
extending his long whip, fairly upset the hat—
when, lo! beneath it appeared a man's head,
not

> " The ghastly form,
> The lip pale, quivering, and the beamless eye,
> No more with ardour bright ;"

but a living, laughing head, by which our inquisitive traveller heard himself saluted with
" Hullo, stranger! who told you to knock my
hat off?" The person thus addressed was so
utterly astonished as not to be able for a moment to understand that the apparition was no
other than a fellow-creature up to the neck in the

mire ; but he no sooner came to this conclusion than he promptly apologized for the indecorum of which he had been guilty, and tendered his services to the gentleman in the mud puddle. " I will alight," said he, " and endeavour to draw you forth." " Oh, never mind," said the other, " I'm in rather a *bad fix* it is true, but I have an excellent horse under me, who has carried me through many a worse place than this—we shall get along." If this story proves the badness of the roads in Ohio, I think it also demonstrates the goodness of the horses and the perseverance of their riders. That it is true, is not for me to assert, as I get it at second-hand —but I will venture to asseverate that it is *as true* as one half of all that has been written in relation to this country ; and if it be in itself but half true, I am privileged as a traveller to relate it.

As a companion to this anecdote, I might relate that of Captain R., who is said to have emerged from a prairie, through whose high grass he had been wading, with five hundred rattlesnakes, hanging by their teeth to each leg ! These things may be so—I have been in the western country six years, and have not seen six rattlesnakes; and I have travelled thousands of miles on horseback, without ever finding the mire so deep that my horse could not keep his head above the surface; but other gentlemen may have met with more adventures.

There is another *snake story*, the relator of which was almost as valiant among these reptiles as Sampson among the Philistines. " I killed a hundred of them," said he, "in a few minutes, each as large as my leg." " I do not dispute it," replied his friend, " but would be better satisfied if you would *fall a snake or two*." " There were *ninety*, I am sure." " Say fifty." "No, I can't; I am convinced there were *seventy-five*, and I'll not bate another snake to please any man!"

We might, perhaps, by adopting a sentiment which is reported to have lately fallen from a judicial bench in New York, say, *these are petty lies, not greater than are told by all travellers;* but if such be the case, I cannot but think that all travellers might *fall a snake or two* with advantage. I have some of their writings now before me, which I wish to notice—because,

although travellers may be privileged to tell
marvellous tales to their friends, I know of no
right which they have to mislead the world by
putting the creations of their fancy into print.

Dr. C. B. Johnson, an Englishman, has written a series of letters to induce his countrymen
to emigrate to a " British settlement" in Pennsylvania; and under an air of great apparent
candour, endeavours to palm on the public the
grossest fallacies. To prove this, it is only necessary to examine some of his arguments. In the
outset it may be remarked, that a writer comes
before the public in a very " questionable
shape," who, professing to furnish an account
of a settlement in Pennsylvania, finds it expedient to slander a country a thousand miles
off, which he has never seen. Pennsylvania is
a rich, extensive, and powerful state, blessed
with a fine climate, and fertile soil, abounding
in mineral wealth, and presenting advantages
to all classes of people; and the author, who
can only eulogize her merits by comparing them
with those of a young republic just struggling
into existence, pays her a poor compliment,
and does little credit to his own ingenuity.

Yet such is the fact. Not content with prais-
ing the spot selected for his own settlement, he
devotes about half his volume to the abuse of
Illinois, and Mr. Birkbeck—because the latter
had written a book which might induce Englishmen to go to Illinois instead of Pennsylvania.
To such a writer it might be sufficient to reply
in the language of Sterne, " Go, poor insect : this
world is wide enough for thee and me."   America has vacant land for all the Britons whom
poverty or disaffection may drive to her shores,
—let them choose where they list—it matters
not.

But let us examine some of Dr. Johnson's
inferences. Mr. Birkbeck mentioned the case
of a " member of a religious community, who,
on being brought before the spiritual court, for
indulging a propensity to boxing, and hearing
all the arguments derived from texts of scrip-
ture, which oppose that unchristian practice,
declared that he would not like to live longer
than he had a right to knock down any man
who told him he lied." Dr. Johnson triumphantly quotes this passage, in support of his
objections against Illinois, and infers from it

" *a proneness to quarrel* in the minds of *the
western people*." The *western people!*—not Illinois merely, but Kentucky, Ohio, Indiana,
Missouri, Tennessee, Alabama, *et cetera!* All
the people of all these states are proved to be
quarrelsome, by the example of one man!
Such is the mode of drawing inferences which
has been practised by the whole mass of English
writers upon America, from Moore the poet,
down to Mathews the player. How easy to
retort such charges! If from the declarations
of a single individual, or his conduct, a " proneness" to any vice, can be inferred to exist in a
whole people, might not " a proneness" to lar-
ceny, in the minds of the people of England, be
inferred with equal truth, from the events of a
single trial at the Old Bailey? But I am most
amused at the idea of an Englishman setting
down our " boxing propensities" in the cata-
logue of objections to us or any of us. They
do not *box* in England, I suppose!—or, perhaps,
their " boxing propensities," are developed in
a more humane and christian spirit than ours.
If I understand the difference, it seems to be
this—that in England boxing is a public diver-

sion, attended by thousands of spectators, not of the "baser sort," but the "curled darlings of the nation," and though against law *in theory*, it is not punished by the law *in fact;* while in this country no boxing is known, except in the rare case, when an individual in the heat of passion resents an affront, as in the instance quoted, and then the law, *in fact*, punishes the assault and battery.   The very anecdote related, if it proves any thing, proves that "boxing" is an offence, for the commission of which an individual is tried; and of course that the policy of the laws, or the moral feeling of the community, or both, are opposed to the practice.   If there is a country in which breaches of the peace are unknown, I have never heard of it ; if there be a country in which men tamely submit to the charge of falsehood, I never wish to hear of it; and if Dr. Johnson had taken any pains to understand the American character, he would have learned that the spirit displayed in the anecdote related by Mr. B. is not peculiar to the West, and that it would not be safe, in any part of the United States, to give the "lie direct."

A A

Having tortured Mr. Birkbeck's anecdote into evidence of "a proneness to quarrelling," Dr. Johnson attempts to give corroborative proof, in an extract from Shultz's travels. Is Dr. Johnson so ignorant of the geography of the United States, as not to know that the country alluded to by Mr. Shultz, and that in which Mr. Birkbeck settled, are separated as distinctly from each other as England and Ireland, and that the people described by these two writers, differ as essentially in their manners, feelings, and propensities, as the inhabitants of those islands; or, is this only another instance of the candid spirit of criticism to which I have adverted? Shultz's travels were written in 1809, and the remark quoted from them, had application to that part of Louisiana, which is now Missouri—a country then recently purchased from France : a country settled, at that time, almost entirely by French, and over which, the mild laws of the United States were hardly yet in operation. Mr. Shultz describes them as a sad turbulent set in 1809, and Dr. Johnson quotes him in 1819 : without adverting to the fact, that the intervening

ten years had essentially changed the population of Missouri, and that at any rate, Illinois
and Missouri are different countries, inhabited
by different people, and governed by distinct
laws. When Mr. Shultz wrote, Illinois was a
wilderness district, appendant to Indiana, with
scarcely the shadow of civil organization, and
almost without white inhabitants; when Mr.
Birkbeck emigrated, it had an organised terri-
torial government, and contained fifty thousand
inhabitants. I presume that the reviewer who
asserts that "a dirk *is* the constant companion
of every gentleman in Illinois," could justify
himself, in a similar manner, under the authority of some traveller into Nova Scotia or
Brazil, and by a reference to the times when
gentlemen were scarce in those regions, and
Indians and wild animals abundant. But let
that pass—we are a quarrelsome people in Illinois, because the people at the lead mines in
Missouri, were so ten years ago, and because
a pugnacious methodist knocked down an un-
polite fellow who told him he lied!

Then we have a caution to emigrants against
going to "the western states, whose infant set-

tlements are *always* exposed to the scalping-knives of the savages!" Illinois, about which Dr. Johnson was writing, is about as much exposed to the Indians' scalping-knives, as Pennsylvania or Great Britain. When Mr. Birkbeck came to Illinois, there was not an Indian tribe or village within a hundred miles of his settlement,* not a *hostile* Indian within thrice that distance. I doubt whether, to this day, the print of the moccasin has been seen in Albion or Wanboro', by Mr. Birkbeck or those who followed him.

The next quotation of Doctor Johnson from Mr. Birkbeck, which I shall notice, is as follows : " children are not baptized, nor subjected to any superstitious rite ; parents name them, and that is all, and the last act of the drama is as simple as the first. There is no consecrated burial nor funeral service : the body is enclosed in the plainest coffin, the family of the deceased convey the corpse to the woods, some of the party are provided with axes and

---

* Except, perhaps, a small tribe of peaceable Delawares on White River.

some with spades, a grave is formed, and the body placed quietly in it; then trees are filled into the grave to protect it from wild beasts. *These simple monuments of mortality are not unfrequent in the woods."* Dr. Johnson italicises the last clause of this paragraph, as if it were pregnant with some sinister meaning; the reviewers have caught at it as a proof of the sickliness of the country; but when I find the intelligent and liberal editor of the Village Record, remarking in allusion to the existence of these " simple monuments"—" it strikes me as quite unusual, and indicates a sickliness of climate justly alarming," I cannot but exclaim, " *et tu Brute !*" The frequent occurrence of graves in the woods, proves nothing; for if the fact be, as Mr. Birkbeck has represented in the first part of this paragraph, that all who die are thus buried, it is hard to discover how, by any possibility, these *simple monuments* can be otherwise than numerous. As all who live must die, the number of dead in any country which has been settled several years, must exceed that of the living, and the number of graves can never afford any proof of

insalubrity of climate: they show how many
persons have once lived, but not when, nor how,
they died.   Mr. Birkbeck's route in the west
lay through Ohio, containing a population of
500,000 souls, Indiana, containing 150,000
souls, and Illinois, containing near 50,000 ; and
if the fact be admitted, upon which these gentlemen build their arguments, that each family
have a separate place of sepulture, the candid
reader may judge how many insulated mausoleums would be presented by such a population,
to say nothing of the vast number of emigrants
and travellers who had preceded Mr. Birkbeck,
and who, like their fellow men, were subject to
the casualties of mortality.

In older communities the burial of the dead
forms a subject of civil regulation.   Places of
public sepulture are provided, or family vaults
are resorted to by those who are able to provide them ; but this is impossible in a country
so thinly populated as a large portion of that
alluded to.   Public grave-yards are not yet
established ; and if I were inclined to draw inferences after the fashion of Dr. Johnson, I
might exclaim, " what a healthy country must

that be where there are no grave-yards!" But
the case is not accurately stated, even in this
instance. It is always to be recollected that
" the western country," is an almost unlimited region, embracing every grade of society
and civilization, from the mere frontier, where
the hunter erects his solitary cabin in the bosom
of extensive forests, where no axe is heard but
his own, where he wages war with the savage,
or mingles with him in the chase, to the polished
circles of Lexington, the crowded marts of
Cincinnatti and Louisville, or the populous and
refined neighbourhoods which are now numerous in almost every western state. In the
oxtromo vergo of society, the hunter who falls
in the pursuit of game, or the traveller who is
assailed by disease in the woods, must lie unburied, or the last act of friendship must be
rudely administered in the manner indicated
above. Such must be the case with the *first*
settlers, the restless pioneers who roam from
place to place, avoiding the contact of dense
population, and depending upon their rifles
for support, and such, in general, must be
the case with those who are the first permanent

settlers in their respective neighbourhoods;
but the barbarous practice—a practice only resorted to in cases of dire necessity—is abandoned
as soon as that necessity ceases. The farmer,
when he becomes permanently settled, clears
and encloses a small spot on his own premises,
as a depositary for the remains of his family; and
it is not unusual to see these spots surrounded
with weeping willows, or hedges of privet or
lilac, which give them a decent air of seclusion,
and testify the respect of the living for the
dead. When a place is thus consecrated, it is
resorted to by all the families connected by
relationship with the proprietor, who reside
sufficiently near, and frequently by all the
neighbours indiscriminately. The next step
in the progress of improvement, is the establishment of public grave-yards, which is usually
effected by religious communities: thus a thick
settlement has its grave-yard. Where the inhabitants are more thinly scattered, every
family has its place of burial, and "the last
act of the drama" is never so negligently performed as is asserted, except in urgent cases.
Still, as there are settlements in which places of

burial are as numerous as families, and as the
traveller is sometimes startled by the sight of a
grave in the wilderness, far from any human
habitation, he who does not reflect upon the
cause, may be struck with the effect.

The former part of the paragraph upon which
I have remarked, is equally incorrect, and exhibits a remarkable deviation from the usual
accuracy of Mr. Birkbeck, whose intentions are
always upright, and whose statements are generally clear and faithful. But he has fallen into
the usual error of those who emigrate from
highly civilized countries, to those which are
less polished, who find the contrast so great
that they do not reflect that it could be greater,
and imagine they have reached the confines
of civilization, when in fact they have barely
emerged from its brightest circles. They fancy
themselves on the frontier, while yet in the
interior, and apply the accounts they have
heard of backwoodsmen, to a race of people
who have but little in common with the genuine pioneers. My respect for the excellent
author of this paragraph, would prevent me
from contradicting any of his statements which

were not directly contrary to the results of my own observation ; but the character of the people among whom my own lot has been cast, requires the refutation of a charge which is anything but honourable to their moral and religious habits—a refutation which I undertake, not because " I love Cæsar less, but Rome more."

In this country then, and in every part of it, the children of professing christians are always baptized, and parents in general endeavour to procure the administration of this ordinance to their children, except in those sects who reject the baptism of infants. It is well known that in some societies baptism is administered only to the children of religious parents, in some only to adults, in others there is less restriction, and some reject the ordinance entirely ; and in the west, as elsewhere, many children are deprived of the benefits of this ceremony, by the negligence or irreligion of their parents : but I know of no habitual neglect of any religious duty, which can be described as characteristic of the western people, or of the people of any state. They are pretty much like others ; better than their enemies believe, and not near so good as their friends could wish. There are many who dwell in secluded situations, where the want of stated ministrations of the gospel is felt as a grievous bereavement; but there is no wilderness so desolate as not to be frequently visited by missionaries and itinerant preachers. Camp meetings abound in every state, and every where draw countless multitudes of people, some of whom undertake long journies on such occasions. "God has not left himself without a witness in the breast of every man."

"There is no consecrated burial nor funeral service"—not because there is no religion, but because our religion does not require this ceremony. In a few denominations only is the burial service practised, and those denominations are the least numerous. There is not a congregation of Episcopalians in Illinois; of Roman Catholics there are a few churches; but the Presbyterians, the Cumberland Presbyterians, the Methodists, and the Baptists, are numerous, and the practice of these christians does not sanction what is called a burial service. The preaching of funeral sermons is more common in the western country than I have ever known it elsewhere. The tribute of respect—if that can be so called, which is intended rather to convey instruction to the living than honour to the dead—is in general paid to the memory of professing christians and their infant children, and it is often extended to others. It is so common as to be no longer a distinction, but rather an ordinary service. I am aware that this is not the kind of funeral service meant by Mr. Birkbeck, but the whole paragraph, taken in any sense, is altogether erroneous.

Mr. Birkbeck advises his friends to bring with them a few simple medicines, and Dr. Johnson *infers* that the country must be dreadfully unhealthy, in which physic constitutes a necessary article of importation. As our author writes M. D., after his name, it might not be unfair to ask him to point out the country which is exempt from disease, or in which medicine is not considered essential to the preservation of life. A mad lover may cry, "throw physic to the dogs, I'll none of it;" but for a sane physician to advocate such a doctrine, would be indeed a

paradox. It is evident, from the whole tenor
of Mr. Birkbeck's writings, that he considered
himself as settled in a perfect wilderness, and
magnified the privations which he expected to
encounter ; and it is true, that in his immediate
neighbourhood there was no physician, nor
apothecary, nor surgeon, nor even a surgeon-
barber ; and knowing that of " all the ills that
flesh is heir to," disease is one of the most inevitable, he thought fit to provide against its
inroads. He had reared a large family, he was
a man of science and observation, and to his
various other attainments, added a respectable
proficiency in the treatment of ordinary diseases. He needed no ghost from the grave to
suggest to him the precariousness of health, to
tell him that "in the midst of life we are in
death," or to convince him of the propriety of
being prepared to combat those evils which
cannot be avoided. He, therefore, in pointing
out to his friends the articles which would be
found most useful, in a country where the arts
had not yet been planted, enumerated medicine,
for the same reason that he designated carpen-
ter's tools, and some other articles which seem

equally misplaced in the outfit of a farmer.
Would not that man be considered as guilty of
a criminal neglect, who should carry his family
into a wilderness where there was no physician,
nor even a Lady Bountiful, without carrying
with him such drugs as would be necessary to
repel those ordinary diseases which assail the
human frame in every climate?

Every ship which is fitted out for a long
voyage is provided with a medicine chest, and
it would be just as fair to *infer* from this
practice the unhealthiness of sea air, as to suppose that Illinois is sickly, because emigrants
are advised to adopt the same precaution.   The
reason in both instances is the same; in both
cases men carry with them that which may be
necessary to preserve life, and which they must
otherwise be without.

A Mr. Lorain, though not a traveller, has
written a book upon the same subject, and
pretty much in the same strain as that of
Doctor Johnson—they use the same ideas and
arguments, and the difference between them is,
that Johnson is the best writer, while Lorain is
the best informed.   The object of both is to

compare Illinois with Pennsylvania, and to refute Birkbeck. Strange! that men should take such pains to compare countries so different in character, and so distinct in their interests—countries between which there is no rivalship, no contact, and no collision! But it seems that a few stray Englishmen, who cannot be contented at home, and who probably would not be satisfied anywhere, may be allured to Illinois by Mr. Birkbeck's letters, leaving behind them the healthful mountains, and fertile vallies of Pennsylvania. If that be all, the controversy is needless—from this class of population Illinois has derived no benefit, and if the whole of it should be diverted to other channels, she would have no reason to complain. Of those already here, the few who have been honest and industrious have prospered; but they bear so small a proportion to the whole, as to leave us but little cause to desire further importations from the same country.

Mr. Lorain, it would seem, has not visited Illinois, and does not pretend to speak from personal observation, but quotes largely from

Volney, and often directs the reader to " *see my book on Agriculture*." What may be the value of the last authority I cannot say, but that of Volney is less questionable. The author who asserts that in the Atlantic states, "the intense heats of the day are usually succeeded by a night of piercing cold"—that "there are few evenings in the year on which fire would not prove agreeable"—that in Philadelphia, "frosts occur, more or less, every month except July"— and at Albany "every month of the twelve," can be entitled to but little credit, when testifying as to the climate of America.

From a long chapter, in which Mr. Lorain attempts to prove the unhealthiness of Illinois, the following passages are selected. "A country being 'new' or unsettled, does not make it sickly, unless the causes that produce diseases prevail in it." This is a truism : for unless the *causes that* produce disease exist, no country, new or old, *can* be unhealthy; but the author's meaning may be gathered from the context. His idea seems to be, that a country is not rendered unhealthy by its being new or unsettled, but by some radical and permanent cause

which is independent of its new and unsettled
state. Mr. Miner is more explicit on this subject: he says, "New countries are generally
healthy ; when they are not so, when diseases
make their appearance with the first settlers,
the climate must be radically bad." This
doctrine is contrary to all philosophy, and all
experience in relation to this subject. The
miasma which creates our autumnal fevers, is
supposed to be produced by the decomposition
of vast quantities of vegetable matter, the undis-
turbed accumulation of ages, which lie buried
in the forests, and in the channels of water-
courses. Mr. Lorain admits this to be the
theory ; and if it be so, it follows that every acre
which is cleared, lessens the quantity of that
matter, the putrefaction of which is alleged to
be the primary cause of disease, because the
deposition of such matter does not take place
upon cleared land, and its accumulation ceases
upon the portion cleared. Upon the first
clearing and tilling of the land, there will be
a more rapid decomposition ; and a greater
quantity of that gaseous effluvia, which is supposed to be pernicious to the human system,

will be created by the operation of tillage, and
the uninterrupted action of the sun and air,
and by these means the cause of disease is daily
decreased. Every furrow ploughed by the
farmer, every beam shot from the sun, every
breeze and every shower, accelerates the process of fermentation, and contributes to neu-
tralize, and evaporate, and at last to destroy the
noxious qualities of that deposit so fertilizing to
the earth, and so poisonous to man. But a
new country has other causes of unhealthiness,
such as are attendant upon a *first* settlement of
the soil, or were pre-existent, and which time
will remove: of these I shall treat more at
large in a separate letter.

"People born and brought up in healthy
countries," says Mr. Lorain, "commonly much
better withstand repeated attacks of diseases,
and live longer in sickly climates, than the
natives." This, with the accompanying remarks, in which the author endeavours to refute
the idea that people may become *seasoned* to
the sickly climate, as he pronounces it, of the
west, is founded in a plausible, but erroneous
theory. The idea is, that the vigorous consti-

tution formed in a healthy atmosphere, will
resist the attacks of disease longer, and more
forcibly, than the debilitated frame reared in
a sickly climate. The premises may be granted
that a strong man may possess a greater tenacity
of life than a weak one, that the one may be able
to resist the same force of disease which would
subdue the other, and still we do not arrive at
the conclusion assumed by the author; for the
doctrine of those who contend that the human
system becomes *acclimated* to a foreign, or even
a deleterious atmosphere, is founded upon the
theory that diseases originating in the climate
do not attack the native, or the person long resi-
dent, with the *same force* which they exert upon
a stranger. It is a wise law of that Providence
which ordained diversities of climate, which
created man with the power of loco-motion, and
adapted him to various spheres of action and
modes of existence, that the human system shall
conform itself to the circumstances under which
it is placed. The infant born under the
equator, receives a different constitution from
that of the inhabitant of the frigid zone; inhabitants of different countries, in the same quarter

of the globe, differ in their corporeal powers
and physical habits; and it is well known that
while sudden transitions from one climate to
another, or violent changes of employment or
mode of life, produce fatal consequences, men
not only become naturalized to foreign climates,
but acquire habits foreign from their nature by
the gradual force of long continued custom.
A backwoodsman will live for a month in the
forest, without seeing a human habitation or a
human face, sleeping every night upon the
ground, with no shelter but the canopy of
Heaven, no protection from cold, but his camp-
fire, no bed but the leaves, subsisting upon
game, sometimes eaten raw, and sometimes
half-roasted, without bread or salt, drinking
often the unwholesome water of rivers, saturated,
as has been described, with the juices of putrid
vegetables, and often enduring thirst as long as
the camel in the desert. It is hardly necessary to
inquire whether the husbandman, accustomed
to a regular life, wholesome food and comfortable shelter, could sustain life long under such
circumstances? The hunter would imbibe
nourishment from the diet which would disgust

his more civilized fellow creature : the one
would enjoy refreshing sleep, while the other
would inhale disease with every feverish aspi-
ration ; like insects of different tribes, the same
food which would afford honey to the one,
would yield only poison to the other.

I must now revert for a moment to Dr. Johnson, for the purpose of shewing another specimen of his style of argument. " The versatility
of disposition, and facility with which an American passes from one thing to another, has
been remarked by every one who has visited
their country. This versatility is very conspicuous in their naval officers. Captain
M'Donough, who took the British fleet on
Lake Champlain, was a merchant ; Captain
Laurence, who, in the sloop Hornet, sunk the
Peacock, was a lawyer ; Captain Jones, who
in the Wasp, took the Frolic, was a doctor ; and
probably most of the others commenced with
some business or profession equally discordant
with their present pursuit." I do not mean to
deny " the versatility of disposition," which
is here very justly attributed to my countrymen, and which I have elsewhere remarked

upon, as the national characteristic; but I do intend to shew the falsity of the proofs by which this writer attempts to support his positions, and his utter ignorance of American affairs. Few of our institutions have been so permanent as the navy : in none has there been so few departures from long established usage. Its improvement, though great, has been gradual ; and its excellence has been achieved, rather by bringing existing principles to their highest perfection, than by any novel discoveries, or bold innovations. That many valuable improvements have been introduced, is true, but they have been built upon immutable bases ; the primary maxims of navigation and naval tactics, the rules of discipline and etiquette, have been tenaciously adhered to.

Among these, no principle has been held more inviolably sacred, than that which obliges every officer to endure a long probation, and to exhibit proofs of merit, previous to his rising into command. To get into the line of promotion, an officer can only enter the navy with the rank of midshipman, and he can only rise by regular gradation. No man has ever risen to the rank of post-captain in our navy since its first establishment, who has not earned that distinction by long and faithful service, in all the inferior grades, with the exception of one individual, whose extraordinary merit was rewarded by an advance of two grades; but this innovation was resented with so much spirit by the naval officers, that the experiment has not been repeated. It is therefore not true that a sudden transition from a civil pursuit to a naval command, has ever taken place in our navy, as would be inferred from the remark quoted, and as *must necessarily be* inferred, in order to give the examples cited any weight as proofs of the general position assumed. "At the age of twelve years," Captain Lawrence is said "to have first discovered a passion for the sea." (See his life in the "Portfolio," for January, 1817.) "But his father, attached to a profession in which he had been considerably distinguished," was solicitous that he should be educated for the bar, and to this solicitude young Lawrence yielded. At the early age of thirteen, he commenced the study of the law, which he pursued for four years.

In the year 1798, at the *age of seventeen*, he received a midshipman's warrant in the navy, and in the year 1813 he became a post captain, after a service of *fifteen* years in the preceding grades. That he understood the *cannon law*, is evident: and he thundered in the ears of John Bull, from the Hornet's deck, arguments which bore no relish of the sophistry of courts; —but I think his history will sustain my *demurrer* to the assertion of Dr. Johnson. The fact with regard to both the other individuals named, is similarly circumstanced; both were destined in early life to other pursuits, but both entered the navy with the rank of midshipmen, and arrived at the high station which they so nobly filled, by long and arduous service.

The example of General Jackson, which our author has stumbled on, is sufficiently in point. This individual has been a lawyer, a judge, a legislator, and a general: and in every occupation to which his versatile genius has been directed, his exertions have been crowned with success. But when the doctor inquires, " what would be thought of one of our judges throwing off his robes and wig and offering to head

an army?" the comparison is idle; there is
no point of similarity. Jackson was a soldier
in his boyhood, a keen sportsman in his riper
years, and through his whole life familiar with
danger, and practised in manly exercises. It
was this unison of mental activity and bodily
hardihood, which produced great men in Greece
and Rome: and the same cause may be cited,
as a reason why our army and navy are not
officered with fool-hardy numsculls, and our
councils swayed by enervated, decrepid patriots.

I shall close this long letter, by examining
the testimony of a witness who is relied upon
as good authority by Johnson, Cobbett, and
others, in their strictures upon Illinois. This
is a man named Hulme, whose " *cacology*"
would have been as grating to the ears of Dr.
Pangloss, as his moral and political principles
are to the feelings of every well regulated mind.
He travels over the mountains in a stage drawn
by *old English horses*, and embarks at Pittsburgh in a boat called an *ark*. His passage
down the river produces not a few eloquent
bursts of indignation against the borough-

mongers, the relevancy of which is not easily seen; but his most profound reflections are elicited by a visit to Harmony. He says, "I observed that these people are very fond of flowers, by the by; the cultivation of them, and music, are their chief amusements; (*these* to me *are a sign* of brute ignorance; at least *a badge* of slavery, they had better have left behind.") I shall not stop to quarrel with the writer's English—I care not whether he writes *these are a sign*, or *these is signs;* but respectfully recommend him to the editor of the Quarterly, who is a capital hand at such matters. But the logic is what I look at: the connection between "brute ignorance and slavery," on the one hand, and flowers and music on the other, is, I confess, not easily discovered. I had thought that th cultivation of flowers, was an elegant employment, the innocent amusement of the gentle and tasteful, a delicate refinement upon the coarseness of rural pursuits. As to music, I can say but little, for I neither fiddle nor sing, and can scarcely distinguish "God save the King," from "Hail Columbia," though I have often felt the sweetness, and acknow-

ledged the power of a "dulcet voice." But
if it be *a badge* of "slavery and brute ignorance," what must be the debased condition of
that people, among whom Madame Catalani
received, in the space of eight years and a half,
more than ninety thousand guineas for benefit
concerts, independent of her receipts for other
exhibitions! How dark the state of a whole
quarter of the globe, if it be true, as has been
asserted, that Signor Rossini, "did more to
agitate, than all the allied powers to tranquil-
lize, all Europe!" I confess that I could not
but smile myself when I read of whole nations
being agitated by the quavering of a fiddle-
stick; but if Mr. Hulme has got the right end
of the story, there is more cause for weeping
than for laughter: Congress should look to it,
and in the next tariff provide against any
future importation of florists or fiddlers. One
thing is certain, that music which has power
"to soothe the *savage* breast," had no effect
upon our traveller, whose breast was too civilized to have any emotions in common with a
barbarian.

At New Albany, he was "amused by hearing a Quaker lady preach to the natives," who "closed with dealing out large portions of brimstone to the drunkard, and larger and hotter to those who give the bottle to drink." "This part of her discourse," he adds, in his usual strain of libertinism, "pleased me very much, and may be a saving to me into the bargain; for the dread of everlasting roasting, added to my love of economy, will, I think, prevent me from ever making my friends tipsy!" It is not without great hesitation, that I consent to soil my pages with the repetition of such obscene ribaldry, such desperate blasphemy; but the hope of contributing to hold up the revilers of my country to the contempt and scorn of the virtuous of every land, induces me to repeat that which I cannot read without disgust.

Between Princetown, and Mr. Birkbeck's, in Illinois, Mr. Hulme says, "we had to cross a swamp of half a mile wide. We were obliged to lead our horses, and walk up to our knees in mud and water." If this be true, I suspect that Mr. Hulme is the first sane man who was ever known to be so fond of grovelling in the

mire, as to dismount from his horse at a time
when the services of that animal were most
requisite. If he had walked upon the hard
ground, and kept his feet dry by riding through
the swamp, his sanity would be less questionable ; but his conduct, as he exhibits it, smacks
too much of the character of that of the man
in the fable, who carried his ass, because people censured him for making the poor ass carry
him ; perhaps our traveller might have received
a similar admonition. " Before we got half way
across," he continues, "we began to think of
going back ; *but there is a sound bottom* under
it all, and we waded through as well as we
could."

The gentleman under the hat, whose sad
predicament I unfolded at the commencement of this letter, found *a sound bottom*
too, but had to go much deeper for it than
Mr. Hulme ; and if the latter had heard this
story previous to his adventuring into Illinois,
he would have known the advantage of having
a good horse under him, and could never have
been induced to quit his saddle under such
circumstances. I incline, however, to the
opinion that Mr. Hulme (if this be not a *nom*

de guerre adopted by some anonymous scribbler) never was in Illinois—certainly, that he never was in *such a fix*, as a woodsman would say, as he describes, or he would have known the advantage of being well mounted on such an occasion, and would never have made this display of his ignorance.

On his travels he, somehow or other, gets into a dancing party, and is highly pleased, as every one who has a spark of human nature in his bosom must be, with the grace, agility, and sweetness of our American girls. Even the barbarous accompaniment of music is forgotten, in the glee excited by the festivities of the young people; but suddenly he finds out that the ladies are clad in British manufactures: and thereupon flies into a tremendous passion, at seeing " the dollars thus danced out of the country into the hands of the borough-mongers, to the tune of national airs !" That which to a genuine Englishman would have afforded a theme of proud exultation, excites only indignation in the apostate bosom of this degenerate Briton. He no sooner recovers his spirits, after this alarming discovery, than his nervous system is again agitated, by an insult which

completely sets forbearance at defiance. He
meets with a person from Philadelphia, who
tells him " a story about *a Mr.* Hulme, an
Englishman, who had brought a large family
and considerable property to America. His
property, the said Mr. Hulme had got from the
British government, for the invention of some
machine, and that now having got rich under
their patronage, he was going about this country doing the said government all the mischief
he could." This charge he repels with suitable indignation ; and completely exhausted with
the rage excited by so dreadful an accusation
as that of having rendered a service to his
country, for which that country had rewarded
him, and of extending his disobedient foot to
trip John Bull's heels from under him, he winds
up with a heroic resolution " to turn Quaker,
or if the Quakers will not receive him"—a qua-
lification which he did well to put in, for I
can assure him the Quakers will not receive any
man, who has so little wit as to lead his horse
through a swamp—" to establish a new society,
which shall have a chairman in place of a par-
son, and the assemblage shall discuss the sub-

ject of the meeting themselves." He concludes
with a fling at the "Cossack priests, the Bour-
bons, and the pope, and exits in a rage!" A
whole volume of such rigmarole, is incorporated
in extenso, by Cobbett, in his "One Year's
Residence in America," and referred to, as
"confirmation strong," of the opinions of that
writer in relation to Illinois.

Almost all the English travellers have been
sadly annoyed by the filthiness of our inns, and
the "myriads of bed bugs" which disturb their
dreams. This reminds me of the quarrels of
our negroes, who seldom fail to stigmatize each
other as "*black* rascals," and is a proof of the
propensity which men have to denounce in
others the bad qualities which are most predo-
minant in themselves. I have never travelled
in England : all my knowledge of that country
is derived from her authors, who fail not to
include cleanliness in the monopoly of virtues
which they arrogate to their nation; but this
I do know, and there are thousands who can
bear me out in the assertion, that if the English
really possess this virtue, they leave it behind
them, when they abjure the realm. The worst

taverns in Illinois have been kept by Englishmen ; and there has never been in this state an inn so badly kept, so filthy, and so extravagant, as has been kept in Albion, by the emigrants from that country.

If the English have found bad treatment at our taverns, it has been produced by their own offensive manners. There is no country in the world in which a well bred traveller will experience more courteous civility, or enjoy more wholesome or neater entertainment, than in ours ; while the kindness and hospitality which he will find in the houses of private gentlemen, cannot but negative the assertion of the poet—

> Whoe'er has travelled life's dull round,
> Whate'er his various course has been,
> Will sigh to think he still has found
> His warmest welcome at an *inn*.

THE END.

LONDON :

SHACKELL AND BAYLIS, JOHNSON'S-COURT, FLEET STREET.

Please remember that this is a library book, and that it belongs only temporarily to each person who uses it. Be considerate. Do not write in this, or any, library book.